The Underdog Advantage

The Underdog Advantage

Using the Power of
Insurgent Strategy to
Put Your Business on Top

David Morey and Scott Miller

McGraw-Hill

New York   Chicago   San Francisco   Lisbon   London
Madrid   Mexico City   Milan   New Delhi
San Juan   Seoul   Singapore   Sydney   Toronto

The **McGraw·Hill** Companies

    4 5 6 7 8 9 0   IBT/IBT   0 9

ISBN 0-07-143919-6

McGraw-Hill books are available at special quantity discounts to use as premiums and sales promotions, or for use in corporate training programs. For more information, please write to the Director of Special Sales, Professional Publishing, McGraw-Hill, Two Penn Plaza, New York, NY 10121-2298. Or contact your local bookstore.

   This book is printed on recycled, acid-free paper containing a minimum of 50% recycled, de-inked fiber.

For Denise, Tyler, and Brett. SM

For Mom and Dad, who taught me to fight like an underdog.
DM

Contents

Acknowledgments

It would be impossible to make a complete list of those deserving thanks for helping us develop the principles in this book. For many years we have been in the remarkable position of being paid to learn. Our clients and colleagues have taught us a great deal. Special mention must go to the late David Sawyer of Sawyer/Miller Group, whose understanding of the information revolution provided the opportunity to build a company based on change. And we would like to single out our friend Sergio Zyman, a true business revolutionary and great mentor (to whom a client once paid the ultimate compliment of describing him as "our *insultant*").

We would like to thank our tenacious agent, Jim Levine, for organizing this book, Leonard Mayhew for suggesting it, and Mary Glenn for editing it. Special thanks go to Janice Race, Joe Michenfelder, Edgar House, George Conyne, Joel McCleary, Max Maven, and Kate Walker Gray for their editorial suggestions. And we could not have produced this work without the excellent case study research of Dan Fields, Mark Mawrence, and Ira Callier.

Finally, we are as smart as our political, governmental, and corporate clients have made us. So eternal thanks go to each and every one of them for teaching us so well about the advantages of being an underdog.

Introduction

How do you plan to succeed in today's superchallenging environment? What's the model? How should you lead your company, your team—even your own career? The current models of corporate and personal management are pretty clearly broken. The advantages of the incumbent seem to have diminished or even disappeared in this brave new world. It's the underdog's day. Whether it's Coke vs. Pepsi or Kerry vs. Bush or Spec Ops vs. Al Qaida—these rules will apply.

This book is about a set of principles that have been proven in political and military action—proven to win and to build a winning attitude, character, and culture in the most difficult circumstances. These are principles that can drive your business, marketing, and communication strategies and transform your company. And they can transform your own career.

This is the underdog advantage: the principles of insurgency, the rules of the revolutionary. Established and refined over centuries of military and political experience, these principles have worked on the battlefield and at the ballot box. This is the spirit that built America and American enterprise. For 25 years, our business has been applying these principles globally to corporate strategy. We've used them to develop competitive strategies, crisis solutions, and cultural changes.

In the late 1970s and early 1980s, we were part of a remarkable revolution, a revolution that changed literally everything within the grasp of human endeavor: politics, business, education, entertainment, science, the arts, media, culture, warfare, and sex. It was the information revolution.

We were able to be there at the start because we were part of a remarkable little company called the Sawyer/Miller Group. It was a company that developed political campaign strategy, but that saw the model of political strategy as having much, much wider application— because that model was shaped around the dynamics of the information revolution. We learned the principles and tactics of that revolution up close, in the world's most electric political campaigns. In the United States, we traditionally worked with Democrats. But globally, we worked with democrats—often democratic revolutionaries who were willing to risk everything for change in Asia, the Middle East, Eastern Europe, Latin America, and Africa.

In the 1980s, we ran international campaigns in countries from Latin America to Eastern Europe to the Middle East to Asia and for candidates from Corazon Aquino in the Philippines to Boris Yeltsin in Russia to Shimon Peres in Israel to Kim Dae Jung in South Korea. It was a remarkable learning experience. And this period of the most sweeping democratic political change in all of history presaged the changes that every business faces today. Corporations, military groups, and indeed all institutions must learn to operate in the hypercompetitive, all-or-nothing, instant-communication world of politics.

In 1984, as we were riding the wave of the information revolution's exponential power, the Coca-Cola Company's Sergio Zyman approached our company to ask: "Can we reelect Coke to the White House? Can we apply the same technique, tempo, and emotion that win a political campaign? And can we use this approach to beat Pepsi?" Later, Apple's Steven Jobs and Mike Murray offered us the same challenge: "Can you help Apple challenge IBM?"

Until then, we had been thinking exclusively about the marketing of politics. But these companies helped us develop a political

model of marketing. And, over two decades, working with some of
the world's best corporate thinkers, we've learned two central lessons.

*First, the rules of leadership, business, and communications
have completely changed.* The old rules are gone. Today's consumers—think in terms of consumers of information, as they may
be customers, employees, or investors—are empowered with
instant and ubiquitous information. These consumers have infinitely more choices. And brands have infinitely more competition.
And all of us are inundated by a tsunami of information—with the
crassly trivial and critically important swirling together in a crashing, constant wave.

As a result, consumers of information feel overloaded. But, at
the same time, they are compulsively seeking even more information.
Today, the tried-and-true rules of mass marketing have been tried and
are no longer true. Greater marketing investments are yielding lesser
and lesser results. There must be a new model for marketing in this
new age. *The Underdog Advantage* provides a new set of rules.

Second, insurgent marketing and communications works. If
you read today's business pages, you'll realize that there are two kinds
of companies and behaviors:

- *Incumbents,* who are bloated, slow, cautious, bureaucratic,
  change-resistant, and more likely to play "defense" than
  "offense" to maintain their power.
- *Insurgents,* who harbor an attitude of difference, move faster,
  and welcome change as opportunity. These insurgents
  embody Alabama football coach Bear Bryant's recruiting
  profile: "mobile, agile, and hostile."

In the end, we find that America's largest corporations are at
their best when they act small—not as arrogant incumbents, but as
hungry insurgents. This is true of clients such as the Coca-Cola
Company, Microsoft, Nike, News Corporation, Disney, McDonald's,
Texas Pacific Group, and Verizon in their moments of greatest success and growth. In this book, we'll analyze this success model and

show, too, how even these great companies often stray from the insurgent path and face the consequences.

Over the years, we have delivered our "underdog advantage" speeches and training to many of the country's most successful corporations. We've preached a prejudice for "playing offense" and empowering individuals or teams with a personal competitive advantage in a world of constant change and challenge.

Uniformly, the reception has been enthusiastic. But adoption of the principles is no slam-dunk. This isn't "Seven Days to Perfect Abs!" This is about changing the way you and your company think, plan, and act. And we have to admit to a failure rate of about 80 percent (not remarkably, that's the same as the failure rate for new businesses and new brands in today's competitive markets). Importantly, while these principles can benefit anybody, they're obviously not for everybody. But those who adopt them succeed.

This book is our "how-to" for developing hyperaggressive marketing, communications, and competitive strategies—for developing the culture of the insurgent, the underdog . . . the only successful business model for the foreseeable future of fast-paced change. It presents the insurgent strategy's key concepts and describes how to develop them into effective tactical planning for any company of any size in any market position. It shows how to develop more effective strategies and create a much more positive and effective attitude and culture within your own organization.

The Underdog Advantage will show you how to:

- Instill the kind of insurgent behavior found inside today's most highly competitive and successful organizations and individuals.
- Promote insurgent strategic planning and execution in every aspect of your company's operations and communications.
- Create a spirit of innovation in your company that leads not only to new product development, but also to new and different approaches to every aspect of your operation.

- Expose individuals to new ways of thinking and infuse them with insurgent principles that they can apply to daily leadership, business, and communications challenges.

In offering this user's manual for aggressive strategists, we draw on our work with notable revolutionaries from business and politics, including Apple Computer's Steven Jobs and Mike Murray; Mexican President Vicente Fox; Microsoft's Steve Ballmer, Bill Gates, and Hank Vigil; Korean President Kim Dae Jung; Coca-Cola's Sergio Zyman; Texas Pacific Group's David Bonderman; Verizon's Ivan Seidenberg; News Corporation's Rupert Murdoch, Peter Chernin, Chase Carey, and David Hill; and, of course, the inimitable fighter who taught us best about courage under fire, Gerry Hsu of Avanti. These leaders shun the role of incumbent—they think and act like challengers, even with the power of leadership behind them.

The key lesson to take from these market leaders is not the traditional corporate cliché of "act like a leader," but rather to continue acting like the hungry, scrappy little company that fought its way to leadership in the first place. And the same thing goes for individual success as for corporate success. The same principles apply. Developing a revolutionary culture begins in the mind and heart of the individual. And this guide will serve as a success road map for you, your work group, your division, your company, or your army.

The age of incumbent power is over. The burden of leadership has never been greater. This is the age of insurgency.

1

Adopt the
Political Campaign Model

"Diplomacy is the art of saying 'Nice Doggie' until you can find a rock."

—WILL ROGERS

➢ *Focus your organization on delivering the win, the whole win—and nothing but the win.*

➢ *Develop an idiot-proof strategy that delivers the win.*

➢ *Create a more results-focused, aggressive spirit in your company.*

➢ *Start kicking ass in the market for a change.*

For 20-some years, we've been teaching our clients to develop business and marketing strategies based on the political campaign model. In fact, our company, Core Strategy Group, is named after the strategic center of every political campaign. In this chapter, we'll show you why and how you should develop this model in your company or group.

Today, you've got more competition than ever before and less room for error. Unemployment isn't just for the working stiffs anymore—in the past 2 years the unemployment rate among *Fortune* 500 CEOs has been running about quadruple that among their employees. A dozen or so of these CEOs are looking forward to several years of tending the garden in minimum-security facilities. You've got to deliver the goods . . . the real thing.

THE POLITICAL INSURGENT CAMPAIGN MODEL

Welcome to political reality: There are no excuses on the morning after Election Day.

That first Tuesday after the first Monday in November in any election year is the all-or-nothing day in politics. One side is picking out carpeting for the West Wing; the other side is returning rental furniture from a dingy campaign office. It's White House or outhouse.

For us, that's the adrenaline rush of politics. *There are no equivocal results*—you win or you lose. If you get 49.9 percent, you take a hike. When a business plan misses its objectives, you hear, "It was a solid year, but due to the bad weather this spring . . . er . . . " And it's on to the next PowerPoint slide.

That doesn't cut it in politics. You win or you lose.

- *Victory is mighty sweet. But it's the bitter taste of loss that you never forget.* You remember that increasingly tight knot in the pit of your stomach that woke you up early on election morning. You looked at the poll numbers, which had been sliding ever so slightly for the past 3 days, and the knot tightened. It didn't get any looser during your fifth cup of bad coffee, any more than it did during the 3 hours of tossing and turning that you did at that Motel 6 the night before with Fox News Channel flickering ghostly light into your restless half-sleep. You listened to anxious reports from the field all morning, with TVs and radios on all over the office. Everybody was on the phone to someone; half of them were trying to set up their next campaign gig. And, sometime around midnight, you were sloshing through a quarter-inch of stale beer in some rented hall, accepting consoling pats on the back; people were telling you, "We'll get 'em next time," but they were thinking what a complete, utter, unbelievable, pathetic loser you are.

These stakes focus the efforts of every political campaign. If you didn't get 50.1 percent or better on Election Day, you didn't have "soft results in the third quarter"; you lost. We've been lucky enough to win a lot and win some big ones in politics and business. But we've lost, too. And it's the loathing of the loss that drives anybody who's been around politics for any time.

Now, think about it. How might your company perform if your people took that kind of attitude toward equivocal results? What if your employees truly hated to lose on even *one* business objective? What if business plan reviews had to answer a simple question: "Did you win—or did you lose?"

You can see why we've built a business by adapting the political model to business competitions.

Our political consulting firm, the Sawyer/Miller Group— founded by the late, great David Sawyer—was the most successful and largest in history. It was sold in 1989 to a fish that was then consumed by a bigger fish and again by a still bigger fish and is now part of the Interpublic Group of Companies. In the 1980s and 1990s, the company surfed the worldwide wave of democratic revolution with candidates like Corazon Aquino, Vaclav Havel, Lech Walesa, and Kim Dae Jung. We won an overwhelming percentage of the senatorial and gubernatorial races in this country that we participated in (and, adhering to truth in labeling, lost two presidential elections on the Democratic side).

In 1984, as mentioned in the introduction, two corporate clients came to us coincidentally with the same request: "Help us think about our business competition as if it were a political campaign." The two companies were Apple Computer and The Coca-Cola Company. Mike Murray and Steven Jobs at Apple and Sergio Zyman at Coke asked us to provide a "political" strategic view of Apple vs. IBM and Coke vs. Pepsi. In truth, at that time, these leaders were way ahead of us in understanding that the principles of political strategy can be transferred and applied to business competition. In fact, not only did they have to explain this to us—they had to teach it to us. Sergio wanted to sharpen the competitive strategies and instincts of his people at Coca-Cola/USA. And Steve and Mike wanted to develop a complete ideological model—and so we worked with and learned from the brilliant political strategist Pat Caddell to create one.

- *IBM was the Autocracy Model.* IBM required you to learn the *machine's* language, which at the time was DOS. This Autocracy Model assumed that your machine would be plugged into a bigger machine and then into the *big* machine (IBM saw the personal computer as only a tiny working part of its "big iron" mainframe computers). In this Autocracy Model, the machine defines your productivity in terms of efficiency and speed. And, to Steve, this Autocracy Model amounted to Big Brother's domain in *1984*. (Lee Clow's famous "1984" Super Bowl commercial for Apple, often considered the best television commercial of all time, promised that the Mac would make sure that "1984 isn't *1984*.")

- *Apple was the Democracy Model.* Its premise was to ensure that the machine learned *your* language, which was Mac OS. In the Democracy Model, your machine was free-standing— in fact, it didn't even have networking capability at the time. According to the Democracy Model, your productivity is defined in terms of your creativity and individuality of thought and expression.

From those two corporate clients, we've gone on to work with Microsoft, News Corporation, Verizon, The Tribune Company,

CitiGroup, The Home Depot, Disney, 7 Eleven, Cox, King World, McDonald's, Highfields Capital, The Boston Beer Company, Visa, KPMG, Nike, Texas Pacific Group, Miller Brewing, Allied Domecq, and many other companies. And, in every case, we've established the political campaign model as the foundation of our work.

While we've continued to refine the model, we've stuck with the basics for two reasons:

1. *Nobody doesn't get it.* It's a simple model. It's easily understood at every level of an organization. In fact, you can find examples of its principles at work (or abused) in every day's newspaper. And, as Henry Kissinger once said, "It has the added advantage of being true."

2. *It works.* Insurgent political strategy was made for today's challenging business environment. The political campaign model clearly frames your company's objectives. It focuses your people on winning. It creates a bolder, more aggressive spirit. And it drives the organization to settle for nothing less than a win over the competition. Moreover, it creates an "Election Day" finish line in terms of getting results.

"But in an election, it's all over after Election Day," you say. "In our business, we've got to keep going . . . we have to sell stuff every day."

That's true. But you've still got elections . . . you have more of them and more often. In fact, *every strategic goal in your company should have its own Election Day*—and the results should show that it either "won" or "lost" on that day. You may have 5 or 10 or 50 strategic initiatives going on at any time, but all of them should be treated as "must-win" situations, as separate campaigns. That means that every one of these strategic imperatives should be developed using the campaign model. Think about it: Should you or your people be doing something that isn't a "must-win"?

Consider your situation right now. Is your company in a competition that it absolutely *must* win? If not, you're working for the government. Are you developing a strategy that *must* get results? If not, your boss is named "Daddy." Are you facing challenges unlike those that you've ever faced in the past? If not, you just haven't wakened to smell the Starbucks. Are you under attack—legal, regulatory, product problem, shareholder, competitive, or internal political attack? If not, watch your back.

Chances are that you're in the campaign mode . . . whether you realize it or not.

Abraham Lincoln challenged his War Cabinet this way: "As our case is new, then we must think anew and act anew."

The same is true today. These are not just tough times; they're very different times. And such times call for a very different approach—the insurgent political approach. But, importantly, while this insurgent political approach may be very different, it's not new. In fact, it's been used successfully for centuries by revolutionaries across the globe in politics, war, and business.

This is what drives the strategies and tactics of U.S. Spec Ops military units, the British SAS, and many of the most effective terror organizations worldwide. This is what drove America's own revolutionaries: Jefferson, Adams, and Washington. And this is what drives the insurgents who rule U.S. markets today: Starbucks Coffee, Wal-Mart and Southwest Airlines; Bill Gates, Rupert Murdoch, Charles Schwab, and Oprah Winfrey. What do they have in common? They have boldness, an outsider's perspective, curiosity, and imagination. They also have classic insurgent leadership skills, planning, and tactics.

This is not the only way to win. Overpowering force still wins very often—although, certainly, a lot less often. It rules many countries. And it still dominates many markets. But today, overpowering force is a very expensive way to win. And it's getting more expensive all the time. Insurgency is simply becoming the most effective and efficient way to win.

Next you ask: "We're the market leader. How in the hell do we *not* act like the incumbent?"

The answer is that *you must make a commitment not to act like the incumbent,* no matter how overwhelmingly you may dominate your market. Insurgent strategies, in fact, will not only help you continue to gain ground, but will also help you develop more satisfied customers and happier, more productive, and totally committed employees.

During the 1980s and early 1990s, Microsoft managed to "lead from behind" in its markets. The company simply didn't accept the role of market leader. Some say that Bill Gates's natural paranoia is part of the company's DNA—and that may be true. But the company carefully and purposely developed the culture and work ethic of the underdog, the revolutionary.

For example, in the early 1990s, Hank Vigil, still a Microsoft stalwart today, was responsible for Microsoft Excel's assault on the spreadsheet market leader, Lotus 1-2-3. To this day, Hank's internal phone line ends with "123" as a commemorative and a reminder of the spirit of that quest. You may well have forgotten Lotus 1-2-3 (more power to Hank's achievement), but back then its market share was somewhere north of 80 percent. Vigil sealed his reputation at Microsoft when he held one of his key insurgent strategy meetings at the Cambridge, Massachusetts, restaurant Michaela's, which, at the time, was in the lobby of Lotus's corporate headquarters building— inside the belly of the beast.

Microsoft succeeded by maintaining the role and culture of the revolutionary. It sustained that culture long after it became a market leader in operating systems and most of the applications categories in which it did business. The PC revolution was its core motivation. In those days, the company mission statement was, "A computer on every desk and in every home." And, remember, this is a company that never did and never will make a computer. It was, and in most ways still is, a company of insurgents: revenge of the nerds.

The danger comes just at the moment when the insurgent is doing high-fives at its victory party. "No more chasing. Now *we're* the effing leader! Let 'em eat *our* dust!"

This is the fatal moment—the moment when the insurgent becomes the incumbent. It's the moment when the insurgent declares victory instead of declaring more war for its noble cause. It's President Bush landing on the aircraft carrier to declare "the end of hostilities" in Iraq. A month earlier, or thereabouts, the United States was pulling down Saddam's statue and had won a victory that stunned the world. Instead of turning incumbent, however, we should have remained insurgent and continued to surprise the world by declaring the join-the-bandwagon global opportunity right there—transferring ownership of Iraq to a coalition including the U.N.: "Come on in and mop up, boys." And it's 5 to 1 that most of the rest of the world would have jumped.

Of course, we have to admit that at times our own clients have been guilty of declaring victory and abandoning insurgency to enjoy all the rights and spoils of incumbency. We'd argue, for example, that Microsoft's worst problems resulted from its taking actions and assuming the attitude typical of an incumbent. In the "old days," Bill Gates delivered an annual speech to the company recommending a new target worth "betting the company" on. The company gambled. And it was an indefatigable pursuer of the bets it made—even when it had already managed to run the table.

In fact, virtually all market-leading companies tend to develop ponderous or even thuggish tactics when they begin to use their leverage over their market partners and dependents to hold on to what they've won instead of betting on the *next* goal. So remember: If you stop playing offense (see Chapter 4), if you stop swimming forward like a great white shark, you're just sinking to the bottom.

RIDING AHEAD OF CHANGE

Today's incumbents must learn to adopt a political campaign model and utilize insurgent strategy. One reason is that the recent recession has obscured seismic changes that have been taking place in U.S., and most global, markets. For most of the past century, the assumption was that the natural tendency toward stability rules all markets. Some called it the principle of regression. Today, however, that is no longer true—instead, change rules. It is change driven by the information revolution. It's the principle of change.

To know is to change. To know infinitely more and know it instantly is to change profoundly. That's what rules markets today. Change rules. And the rules of change greatly favor the insurgent, because the insurgent embraces change and loves change. The incumbent hates change, because change is a threat. Swimming against change these days is flailing against a riptide. As we've said and will say again and again, these are *very* tough times for incumbents.

We see, in fact, two important elements of Big Change.

1. *Big Change 1: The traditional structure of markets is crumbling under the weight of the information revolution.*

Traditionally, virtually all markets have had three tiers:

- *A top tier.* This tier holds two or three nationally known, mass-marketed leader brands. These brands have established the "category brand"—the understood attributes and benefits that define the category. These category brands become the table stakes for playing in this upper end of the marketplace.
- *A middle tier.* This tier holds as many as several dozen "follower" national brands in the slipstream of the top-tier brands. These middle-tier brands tend to all share the same brand positioning: "Me, too!"—the world's most popular brand positioning. They differentiate themselves subtly, often on price.
- *A bottom tier.* This tier holds the zillions of smaller, customized, personalized niche brands—which may be local or regional.

The movement among these three market tiers has traditionally been glacial. Once you reached the top tier, you were almost frozen in place. But today, the information revolution has had the effect of a massive, sudden global warming. And nothing will ever be the same. In fact, the information revolution's effect has been to provide consumers with infinitely more choices in every marketplace and infinitely more information about those choices.

As a result, today's consumers have begun to change the way they move in markets. At present, they are moving in two directions.

First, they are moving to the *top of the market*, to one sure-thing big brand that is guaranteed to be available, affordable, and acceptable. One leader brand is dominating its category more often than in the past half century. And, in most categories, you see the number two and three and four brands sucking wind and often falling into the middle tier (e.g., consider Burger King's and Wendy's relative market losses as McDonald's has gotten its act together).

Second, the same consumers are moving just as strongly to the *bottom of the market* to fill out their personal choice menu with brands customized to their needs and wants. This menu contains one big brand and maybe five or six small brand options. Indeed, most of the vitality and innovation in today's markets is bubbling up from the bottom.

So, then, what does this movement to the top and bottom of today's markets mean?

- *In the process of this movement, we see a crushed middle market.* At present, this middle market is going or gone in every single marketplace in which we work. Indeed, if you want to find that stubborn unemployment in the apparently rebounding U.S. economy, this is where to look. In this crushed middle market, companies have been lost, swallowed up, or dragged into a slow, painful, layoff-inducing decline.

- *Today, most life is found in just two market tiers: the top tier and the bottom tier.* And the brands in the top tier go to market very differently from the brands in the bottom tier. Moreover, brands in the middle tier have generally held on to their own imitative and lower-rent versions of top-tier marketing for too long.

- *If you intend to play at the top of the market, you must bring buckets of money*—more and more all the time, in fact. This is marketing on a mass scale in every way. This approach has defined America's and the world's most successful brands for most of a century. But this, too, is changing.

- *In the bottom tier, desperation and high-stakes poker define marketing.* This is what the experts have termed, with derision, "niche" marketing. But this niche marketing has been increasingly successful with consumers who are relatively sophisticated and cynical—which is to say *all* consumers today. Consider the success of Google or Starbucks or Jet Blue or Krispy Kreme or Linux. Their marketing has been nontraditional and nonmass to such a degree that the famous marketing experts have incorrectly defined it as "un-marketing." But, it's more correctly identified as non-mass marketing—what we call insurgent marketing. This is not a lack of marketing strategy; it's simply a radically new marketing strategy.

- *The growing success of marketing for brands in the bottom tier depends directly on the diminishing success of marketing for brands in the top tier.* This isn't just the zero-sum equation of markets today. Rather, this insurgent marketing depends on growing consumer savvy and cynicism about mass marketing's tired tactics; consumers of all ages are on to the game. It's like the big brands are playing three-card monte with just two cards. And, these days, the suckers always know where the ace is, but sometimes they simply choose to lose, for personal convenience or out of whimsy. They choose to fall for mass marketing occasionally, whether they believe it or not. (For example, the last Yankelovich Trend Research report we saw indicated that mass broadcast advertising has a credibility level of about 6 or 7 percent—amazingly, it's more than 90 percent unbelievable.)

This crumbling of the traditional market structure and movement to the top tier and the bottom tier makes marketing the biggest brands increasingly expensive—even as they dominate their markets more and more. Of course, according to generally accepted economic theory, it just isn't supposed to be that way. So, what's up with that?

2. *Big Change 2: The big are getting bigger. But the rich are getting poorer.*

What happened to economies of scale? Today, the top-tier brands are spending more than ever to make every single sale—even as their market domination increases. Their top-tier competition may be getting weaker, but their customers' resistance is getting stronger. And it's the orneriness of consumers—in everything from complex financial instruments to fast food—that's spoiling the game for the big guys. Customers aren't playing nice. Imagery—a euphemism for B.S.—is not getting the job done.

More and more, the big marketers are turning to the one mass marketing tactic that still moves consumers: price promotion. In our terms, they're buying votes and paying more and more for them every election. And, of course, consumers are acting just like voters. When was the last time the pundits called an election correctly? Conventional polling doesn't measure an election's last-minute unpredictability simply because voters don't *want* it to do so. Indeed, it's no accident that our electorate is now divided a third, a third, and a third between Republicans, Democrats, and Independents.

Increasingly, sophistication and cynicism in the marketplace are diluting the effectiveness of every traditional marketing trick and the bag in which it comes. As we'll argue throughout this book, the "one-size-fits-all" proposition of mass marketing—the tube sock of the 1970s was mass marketing's poster child—just doesn't fit anymore. In fact, today's informed consumers are convinced that if they just keep looking, they'll find the "one size that fits just *me*!"

So you've got a double whammy: Mass marketing costs are increasing—and so are product development costs. Today's customers know more and demand more. In fact, *product integrity—how your product or service lives up to its inherent brand promise—is more critically important in this environment than at any time since the beginning of mass marketing*, and maybe since the beginning of marketing itself. As ad pioneer David Ogilvy once said, "Nothing kills a bad product like good advertising."

All this means the digital age's instantly informed and constantly communicating consumers are the most powerful advertising medium in history. They are killing bad products like a giant bug zapper. And, interestingly, brands on the bottom tier are placing their bets on product differentiation. Almost always, these brands and products are founded on a conviction that differentiation will win. And, finally, they're right.

On average, the young male beer drinker can't distinguish between Budweiser and Miller Lite. But he sure as hell can tell a Sam Adams when he tastes one. Boston Beer's founder-brewmaster Jim Koch makes sure of that. He'd rather be rejected because of the taste than ignored because drinkers can't differentiate it. So the insurgent managers on the bottom tier can be just as ornery as their own consumers.

Life in the top tier is getting harder and harder, too. But, fortunately for our national economy, some of the top brands are getting smarter and smarter. They're learning from the success of the bottom-tier brands. They're learning to compete like insurgents, not incumbents. And, as we'll say again and again (and again and again), *when an incumbent market leader learns to compete like a market insurgent, it becomes unstoppable.*

- One great example of a top-tier brand playing by the insurgent rules of the bottom tier is Frito-Lay. After decades of putting its faith in mass advertising, Frito-Lay has put its faith in product—which, of course, strongly implies that it's put its faith in customers. The core of Frito-Lay's marketing is product differentiation, which is in a constant state of development and change. That's because Frito-Lay annihilated its major, mass-marketed brand competition—and because it was forced to turn its attention to the local and niche snack brands that might otherwise have nibbled it to death in guerrilla wars in market after market.

Today, most big companies expect every new product to sustain its early success in a market. Frito-Lay, by contrast, expects product differentiation to have the shelf life of warm buttermilk. It keeps pulling products before consumers get a chance to sense that those products are stale (stale, in terms of having been "seen" or "raised" by competitive options). For the insurgent Frito-Lay, new products mean new forms, new flavors, and new packaging concepts.

Walking the aisles of a New York area supermarket recently, we looked at the 10 yards of shelf space that Frito-Lay controls in the snacks section. Along that 30 feet, we saw a price per unit range of $1 per pound to $9 per pound, although the price-to-consumer range of the products was much tighter. The differences were in all forms of newness—forms, flavor, and packaging concept. The $1 dollar per pound was Lays Classic. Every 5 feet or so there would be a "keeper" brand, flanked by several "temporary" brands. It's the combination of keeper and temporary brands that builds the franchise and Frito-Lay's brand. Frito-Lay has found the supermarket aisle to be the most effective medium of communication for it. And it's hard to ignore the communication because of the constant change of product brands and sub-brands in the displays. It's about the product, stupid. Frito-Lay is all over that concept.

- Toshifumi Suzuki, the visionary of Japan's supermarket chain Ito-Yokado, now owner of America's 7-Eleven, is another example of an insurgent spirit at the helm of a market leader. Suzuki, for example, developed the theory of "dead merchandise" in his tiny 7-Eleven stores in Japan over 20 years ago. In Suzuki's view, if a customer walks past an item on a shelf two or three times without buying it, it's "dead." It's bad. And it can infect the products around it. So he instituted constant inventory turnover in his Japanese stores. Fifteen years ago, Suzuki and 7-Eleven Japan set out to buy up the U.S. company's franchises in Hawaii, simply because they were embarrassed by the impression these stores made on Japanese tourists. At about the same time, they decided to buy the California stores for the same reason, and they found that for the price of these two, they could get the whole damned company, which had been strapped for cash ever since a 1980s leveraged buyout.

Today, whether you're a giant market leader or a tiny new brand holding on by your fingernails, you've got to consider adopting an insurgent strategy—the campaign model—if you want to win in the marketplace. It may sound scary. Many managers wince at our strategies and say, "But leaders don't *do* that kind of thing."

And our answer is always the same: "Oh, yes, they do. It's just that many of them aren't still leaders by the time they get around to doing it."

There is comfort in tradition. But these days you can ride tradition right over the falls. Sometimes the safest thing to do is the scariest: Jump. You know you must change the way you do things—the only questions are how and when.

INSURGENT BOLDNESS WINS TODAY

Think about your company in very personal terms. Are your greater personal regrets for the things you did or the things you *failed* to do? Are your greater regrets for the path taken or the one *not* taken? "Be bold," Goethe said, "for there is magic in it."

Just do it. Here's why:

- *Make it happen.* This isn't Zen; you can't just "let it happen." It's time to fish or cut bait in the zero-sum competition of today's markets. First and foremost (and we're going to keep repeating this until it's burned into your hard disk), the insurgent strategy works. It gets to the solution, which is winning. By the way, winning is fun.

- *Frame the project.* Using the political model clearly shows your people how to think about any challenge facing them. They must win—that is, they must deliver the objectives. They must win by "Election Day." And they must move key "voters" in order to win. This will force you, the boss, to create a very crisp and clear definition of winning . . . and force you to create realistic, achievable goals.

- *Focus your people.* Your group will operate more effectively and efficiently when it's driven by an "Election Day" focus. People will understand what it means to win (and to lose) and what they must do to win the votes that will turn the election. They'll wake up every morning knowing whose votes they have to win that day. Churchill said: "Nothing focuses the mind like knowing you're going to be shot in the morning." We'd amend that to: "Nothing focuses the mind like knowing who you have to shoot in the morning." Point your people at the enemy.

- *Energize your company's work.* Playing to win, not just to survive or to deliver marginal results, is highly motivating in itself. If you don't keep score, why play?

- *Create an aggressive, iconoclastic insurgent culture.* The very same professionals who put their candidate in a tank and ran the disastrous Dukakis campaign in 1988 ran the "Comeback Kid" war room for Bill Clinton in 1992. *Question:* What was the difference? *Answer:* The insurgent nature of the campaign's leader, Bill Clinton.

    IBM under Lou Gerstner was a completely different company from IBM under John Akers. *Question:* Given that Gerstner didn't fire every one of his reports and that the preponderance of the thousands of IBM employees also worked for Akers, what was the difference? *Answer:* Gerstner's

JUST DO IT

Adopt the political campaign model. It's the only winning formula in a world of change.

- Focus your organization on delivering the win, the whole win—and nothing but the win.
- Develop an idiot-proof strategy that delivers the win.
- Create a more results-focused, aggressive spirit.
- Start kicking ass in the market for a change.

Steps

- Adopt the reality of a campaign.
- Define "Election Days" for every business objective.
- Model insurgent leadership.
- Prepare your change map. Figure out where you—and your competitors—are. Commit to changing the dialogue in your market.

Exercises

- Spend a full day inside a political campaign 1 week before the election. Or visit the field of the winningest athletic coach you can find within 2 hours of your home. Absorb the best example of an insurgent culture that you can find.
- Who is the insurgent political or business leader you admire the most? What does this leader do? How does he or she act? How does he or she prioritize? How does he or she always stay on the attack?
- What victories must you win? What voters must you move? What are your three core objectives? And what's an Election Day at least 12 months in the future on which you can focus your entire organization and its resources? Write this out across a 12-month calendar and sell it to your organization's leaders.
- Brainstorm and list 10 or more small, doable things that you can do over the next 3 months to reenergize your product or service. Prepare a prioritized schedule to get them done.

relentless focus and commitment to culture change. A fellow Southeastern Conference football coach once said of Alabama's Bear Bryant: "He can beat your'n with his'n—then turn around and beat his'n with your'n." That's insurgent leadership.

2

Do the Doable

---

*"The idea is not to die for your country. The idea is to get
the other son of a bitch to die for his country."*
—GENERAL GEORGE PATTON

> ➤ Teach your company to focus on achievable, but no-
> compromise, results—not the same old loosey-goosey
> objectives.
> ➤ Develop "momentum objectives" that teach the mem-
> bers of your team to be winners and create a "success
> culture."
> ➤ Create a spending discipline that is tied directly to
> strategy: "How is this dollar going to win a vote?"

There is one core principle that drives nearly every decision within
a successful political campaign: *Do the doable*. This is in stark contrast to the usual business plans that we've seen over the years, which
seem to follow the quixotic principle "dream the impossible dream."

It's hard to get people in business to define crisp objectives because the definition of winning in business is often so subjective: "We expect to return to double-digit growth." "Our plan is to reverse the brand's slide in the marketplace." "We expect to gain share on the market leader."

That just won't cut it in a political campaign. Nothing less than 50.1 percent is a win. "Almost" means total failure. For example, when we were working with a major U.S. brewery, we attended five or six of the brewery's annual sales conventions. At each meeting, the marketing director (three different ones in the course of the annual meetings we attended) told the audience of beefy beer distributors that results were "a little disappointing" because of the rainy spring that year. Amazingly, in all of these annual meetings, nobody once raised a hand to ask, "Didn't it rain on the competition, too?" Or "Doesn't it rain *every* spring?"

If a campaign worker wakes up to a driving blizzard on Election Day, that worker just straps on the snowshoes: She or he still has to deliver the votes. "Almost" is abject defeat. Ask Al Gore.

It's hard to get people in business to deliver strategic objectives for the simple reason that the consequences of failing to deliver are so mild. "Almost" is good enough. That encourages setting even *more* unrealistic goals. After all, unrealistic goals make for a happy planning meeting. They sound so robust and promising. They make the volcano gods happy: The boss smiles. Nobody wants to hear that you're planning another mediocre year. And 12 months later, you can always look into the bleakest darkness of results and find some ray of hope: "We did much better in the South Central Region," or "We gained some real traction in the Hispanic market."

On a losing election night, announcing, "We did much better in the South Central Region" wouldn't be heard over the boos.

But maybe you've noticed that your business dynamics have been getting a lot more like politics lately. These days, it's a lot harder to get the volcano gods smiling. It's a lot harder for a CEO to get a smile out of the board, out of analysts or investors. Chances are that your CEO has to sign his name to the company's financial results. Five years ago, he might have simply turned to his CFO and said, "Fix it."

Today, the only "fix" is real results. There are the new accounting and auditing standards known as Sarbanes-Oxley. There are CFOs in handcuffs. So today it's about real results, which makes it a lot more like a political campaign (minus the lead sandwiches and bad coffee). Business is focused on performance now—not buzz, glitz, or excuses.

In this chapter, then, we're talking about practicality, but *winning always begins with practical dreaming*. You've got to have a clearly defined destination in mind, that "shining city on a hill" toward which you and your team keep working. And we'll show you how to get there yard by yard with "do the doable" business planning—but you'll have to start with a look way down the road.

DEFINE THE FUTURE

Before you set business objectives for your next plan, try defining what winning will mean in the broadest, but clearest, possible terms: How is it going to change the future? Most companies call this a mission or vision. And mostly this mission or vision is written in corporate gobbledygook. Any time we see the word *excellence* in a vision statement, our eyes go blurry.

So we'll argue here and again in Chapter 4 that you need to *define the future in detail*. Tell a great story. This is the future that will result if your company, product, or service achieves real success over the next 3 to 5 years. You need to define the future in the context of your customers' lives, because your success will be achieved *only* if your customers achieve the future you have defined. In other words, how are you going to make your customers' lives better?

We've mentioned our favorite corporate mission statement, that from Microsoft in the 1980s: "A computer on every desk and in every home."

We once heard Bill Gates give a speech to a computer industry trade show audience in which he said that he was going to talk for half an hour about what life would be like in America in 10 years, and he promised not to mention even one Microsoft product. Gates then talked about the ways in which life would be easier and work more productive. He described the American home and the American office in terms that made you want to be there. True to his word, Microsoft was never mentioned. But it was understood that this future would be running on a Microsoft platform.

We learned a simple principle from Gates in the 1980s and early 1990s: If you define the most compelling picture of the future, you are likely to be given the chance to shape that future. Competitors will line up behind your definition of things to come. The great story wins.

Learn to define the future in detail. As we've said, most businesspeople don't take this first step very seriously. Mission statements are for the inside cover of annual reports, right? They often become a useless exercise in platitudes. Instead, write a very detailed view of the future and what your role in making that future happen is going to be (again, see Chapter 4). It's not just Gates who's done this effectively; every so-called business revolutionary—Edison, Ford, Turner, Murdoch, Milken, and Branson, among others—has done so. Do the best job of defining the future and you'll have the best chance of controlling it.

The same principle operates in a political campaign: The candidate who does the best job of defining for voters "what this election is all about"—that is, what the outcome will mean in terms of defining the future—will almost certainly be the winner. Remember Ronald Reagan's convincing line from his debate with incumbent Jimmy Carter: "It comes down to this. You must ask yourself, 'Are you better off than you were 4 years ago?'"

Reagan is often portrayed as being all about imagery, but that campaign was all about substance. While Carter had defined our nation's difficulties as a national "malaise," Reagan defined them as our greatness struggling for release. To allow this release, he said, we had to do three things: "Get government off your back and on your side; cut taxes to stimulate the economy; and confront the 'evil empire' of Soviet Communism." Nobody could accuse that clear platform of pandering for votes. What you saw was essentially what you'd get.

You're defining the same context for your own employees and other stakeholders: What's this "election" all about; what's this campaign all about? What's at stake? How is this election going to get us to the future we all want . . . to the *big* win … the great story?

The people in your company, even the ones you often call "those disloyal SOBs," want to be a part of something great. They really don't want to just punch a time clock. They want to change the future. For example, in the early 1980s, 99.9 percent of them would have loved to have been hand-picked by Steve Jobs to help establish the Macintosh unit at Apple—to work in a building that flew not only the American flag but the skull and crossbones.

If you adopt "do the doable" planning, you're going to be asking your people to grind out yardage the hard way. You're not going to accept "almost." It won't be easy. But you want their "eyes on the prize," as Martin Luther King used to refer to his vision of the future, defined so beautifully and clearly in his speech at the Lincoln Memorial in 1963. Let your employees be the insurgents. Let them be the ones about whom the competitors ask in frustration and fear, as Butch Cassidy and the Sundance Kid did, "Who *are* those guys?!"

It takes energy and focus to win in markets today. And this comes from understanding that you're a part of a big-picture effort that's going to change people's lives—including your own. But it's fueled by the wins along the way that will get you to that future. Touchdown drives in football are remembered for the first-down plays that got the team to the end zone. And, as an insurgent, you're starting from deep in your own territory. This is not "Hail Mary" territory. You're just trying to move the first-down sticks. *Define goals in a sequence based on order of difficulty*—"do the doable" means "win the winnable" first.

DEVELOP A "DO THE DOABLE" BUSINESS PLAN

To get real results, set achievable goals and develop a "must-win" attitude toward reaching them. But to win, do the doable. Begin with market intelligence, because market stupidity is the alternative—being guided by anecdote, fear, or overconfidence.

In fact, the insurgent must understand its market targets (consumers, distributors, potential market partners, decision influencers, and so on) better than any competitor and far better than the market incumbent, who has probably begun to take its hold on these audiences for granted. Moreover, the insurgent must also understand the strengths and weaknesses of the competition better than the competitors themselves do. And this must involve a starkly realistic assessment—not one shaped by bias, grudges, or hopes.

Often, we do something to mitigate the effects of our natural biases. We develop what we call a "C team" to get into a competitor's shoes and mind and use this perspective to understand the market context on that competitor's terms. As we'll discuss in detail in Chapter 6, we've even sponsored market research by this team as if we were the competitor (and we've discovered that the client who is sponsoring the research often has an important effect on the research company's report of results and analysis).

Things look different from the other side's trenches. Douglas Ivester, Coca-Cola's former chairman, once sent us to a convention of manufacturers and marketers of private-label brands. It was one thing to look at printouts measuring incursions by competitive brands called President's Choice, Safeway Select, or Sam's Choice. And it was one thing to listen to our own people's emotional over- or underestimates of those private-label brands' strengths. But it was quite another thing to be among these market insurgents and sense their zeal. In fact, they did not call themselves "private label" or "store brands" at the time—they called themselves "control brands," because they allowed retailers greater control over their own profits.

The convention's most powerful presentation was from the Canadian supermarket chain Loblaw. Its marketing logic was developed out of the new reality of time-stressed, information-cluttered consumers: 80 percent of brand decisions are being made at the shelf these days—in 6 seconds or less. So putting the store's generic brand on the bottom shelf with none of the quality and value clues provided by product, packaging, and merchandising isn't good enough. You've got to be on a level with the top brands in every way—product delivery, package type and design, label, merchandising, and price—and you've got to be positioned as having top-brand quality or better, but with a price just below that of the top brand. And this realistic view of its friendly competitors—who, by the way, were also its best customers—helped Coca-Cola develop its own insurgent strategy against the control brands.

So winning today requires a clarity and realism superior to that of the market incumbent. And with such a clear and realistic view, you can start planning.

- *The first rule of "do the doable" is "don't break your pick on the impossible."* Don't even think about objectives that are impossible to reach. That simply dilutes your credibility and demoralizes your people. As a recent business ad says, "Hope is not a strategy." Think about success in terms of a set of steps that will lead to a big, but achievable, win.
  - Will that success depend on continuous product development? And which developments are most realistic to achieve?
  - Will that success depend on achieving a certain level of distribution or opening a new channel?
  - Will that success depend on hiring a new regional sales manager?
  - Will you roll that success across several geographies?

  And so it goes—list all the elements of your success as objectives, even if that means listing 10 or 15 objectives for your plan instead of the traditional three or four. List them in order of difficulty (see the next item). You want to teach your people to fight one battle at a time and win each one.

- *Establish your objectives in order of difficulty.* Knock off the easiest (most winnable) ones first. There's a football principle that was boomed out over Washington & Lee University's practice fields by Coach Boyd Williams: "Take what they give you!" If they give you the off-tackle play, keep running it until they take it away. If they give you the short pass, keep throwing it until they take it away. It's great advice—analyze the marketplace in terms of competitive "gimmes." Where are the weak points in the market leader's product, placement, distribution, customer service, and so on? What has the market leader left uncovered? Importantly, when you take what they give you to get a market foothold, you force the market incumbents to change strategy and decide whether to confront you. You create energy and focus for your people and anxiety and sometimes redeployment for the incumbents.

    Many a new and insurgent brand finds its opportunity in the seams ignored by the big incumbent brands. For example, Arizona Iced Tea wanted placement in stores anywhere *except* on the soft drink aisle. And today, it's ended up with three or four placements—near bottled waters, near bagged teas, near juices, and sometimes off on its own. In fact, Arizona Iced Tea helped to create a "new age" beverage display category in many stores (and immediately started trying to break out of there). Moreover, Arizona Iced Tea didn't follow the leaders on packaging, either; it pioneered a 20-ounce can, as opposed to the standard 12-ounce cans and 16-ounce bottles. And the company continually experiments with the guiding principle of differentiating Arizona Iced Tea from traditional soft drinks. By doing so, Arizona Iced Tea's people have achieved a lot of "wins"—rewarding the company with an insurgent reputation in the marketplace. And, most importantly, this strategy has given Arizona Iced Tea a share of the bottled iced tea market that challenges that of the incumbent leaders, Nestea and Lipton.

The energy drink Red Bull didn't even *try* to break into supermarkets. Instead, it established a market foothold in liquor stores, which had plenty of elbowroom for a soft drink on their shelves. And there was plenty of room on the beer trucks that were delivering the brand. Furthermore, soft drinks seldom emphasize their ingredients—but that's exactly how Red Bull achieved its differentiation. Also, soft drinks seldom emphasize the fact that they are used as mixers in alcoholic drinks. But Red Bull established its urban legend first in Europe and then in dance clubs in New York, Los Angeles, and San Francisco. When mixed with vodka or champagne, it was a way of helping young people boogie all night. That's right, coach, take what they give you.

- *By establishing your objectives in order of difficulty, you create what we call "momentum objectives."* Winning each one makes the next one easier to win. It's the same in sports: The college powerhouses try to begin their seasons with an easy-to-beat version of what heavyweight legend Joe Lewis once called the "bum of the month." And it's the same as winning presidential primaries in politics: It gives you what "Bush 41" called "the Big Mo." Moreover, it sharpens your strategy and tactics. It teaches winning. It teaches your teams to believe in themselves. And it builds a winning culture: By the time your people get to the really tough ones, they know they can do it—and they know they must. Ten yards at a time, you can reach the toughest goal.

- *Creating momentum objectives also preserves your resources for the harder challenges that lie ahead.* Generally, political campaigns budget from Election Day backward, realizing that up to 60 percent of the budget will be spent in the campaign's last 2 weeks. Today, there are very few brands that can afford to carpet-bomb their way through the markets. You've got to get a lot more out of a lot less. Unfortunately, most business-people adjust to that reality simply by cutting back on the budgets for traditional strategies and tactics. But the best way is to establish new strategies and tactics for this new reality. Scaling back, in fact, is simply a form of retreat—and retreat is the most difficult military maneuver. Furthermore, this provides the most often used excuse for poor performance: "They cut our budgets." So, don't retreat; rethink (more about creating this rethink ethic later in this chapter).

To recap "do the doable" business plan objectives:

1. Define more objectives that are more achievable. Go for first downs, not touchdowns.
2. Never list an objective that you can't reasonably achieve.
3. Set your objectives in order of difficulty, not in order of importance.
4. Develop momentum objectives and create a culture of success.
5. Create a take-what-they-give-you attitude toward identifying achievable objectives.
6. Rethink—don't retreat.

SHOOT DOWN THE BLIMP

Doing more with less is the reality of all business planning today. Never just cut back—instead, zero-base your objectives and strategies to create a new plan for a new reality.

Develop a political campaign manager's attitude toward spending. Whether it's on the scale of a multimillion-dollar presidential campaign or a local city council race, the spending discipline that manages winning campaigns asks perpetually: "How is spending this dollar going to help win a vote, much less this election?"

Now, to exemplify this point, we're going to get onto a *very* touchy subject: corporate sponsorships as marketing tactics. One of the most wretched of the wretched excesses of the dot-com craziness was buying stadiums as a way of proving that you could play with the big guys. "It's $32 million," one dot-com CEO told us about buying a name change for Foxboro Stadium, home of the New England Patriots, "but it's just a million a year for 32 years."

Actually, it would have been a million a year for only 1 year, since the dot-com in question went belly-up. But take a look around the NFL, NBA, MLB, and NASCAR: "Invesco Stadium." What in hell were they thinking? "Hey, Dan, in between quarters, why don't we head up to the refreshment stand and buy some mutual funds?"

There may even be a curse involved in this madness. Wasn't "TWA Dome" the dying gasp of that airline in its St. Louis hub? Even for a consumer goods company, what do these sponsorships buy you? We're often told that such sponsorships allow a company to entertain top clients in real style. But what about TicketMaster? Can't you just buy the tickets or buy a corporate box instead of buying the stadium—or the stadium scoreboard or clock?

Think of the blimps at every sports event and the giant product inflatables at every convention. Our friend Sergio Zyman tried to confront marketing's outlandishly expensive party favors when he was Coca-Cola's chief marketing officer. What he found was that in a big corporation, every blimp, every product blowup, every racing team, and every stadium sponsorship has a constituency that depends on these excesses for its existence. It's also their social currency; members of these constituencies are in the racing business or the football business, or the blimp business—but not in the soft drink business. And fighting them over a trivial and wasteful expense meant that Sergio was engaged with people who were fighting for their very lives. Still, to know Sergio is to know that he fought the good fight.

This is marketing?

What is the "Official Beer of the NFL"? Budweiser, right? Wrong. That's another problem that's been documented again and again in Olympic sponsorships. Not only are consumers not sure whether your brand is an "official sponsor," but they're also just as likely to credit your competitor's brand with that title and whatever perceived value goes along with it.

In this age of increasingly sophisticated and cynical consumers, what are you really buying with these marketing dollars? Even the youngest kids understand the marketing game very well. They don't think a sports star actually eats the candy bar or soup that he endorses. How silly would that be? And they know that LeBron James will play in high heels if the price is right. In other words, they're onto the game. So what does it win you?

We were once doing market research for a brewery, doing individual in-depth interviews with NASCAR fans who drink a lot of beer. We sat down with a guy in Alabama. He was wearing a black and gold Miller Genuine Draft "Rusty Wallace" T-shirt. He had on a "#19" Miller Genuine Draft "Rusty Wallace" baseball cap. He had more tattoos than teeth. And we asked him the obvious questions first.

"You follow NASCAR?" we asked.

"Yessir," he answered.

"And you like Rusty Wallace?" we asked.

"He's my man."

"Do you ever go to NASCAR races?"

"Every one I can," he answered. "About four every year."

"By the way," we asked, "what brand of beer do you drink?"

"Busch," he replied.

And then, seeing our wondering faces, he asked, "Why?"

"Well, Rusty Wallace drives for the Miller Genuine Draft racing team," we suggested.

Our interviewee gave us a look like we were a little dim on the subject of NASCAR, as we asked, "Don't you think you should drink Miller Genuine Draft?"

He seemed to think this might be a trick question, but he answered, "No . . . why?"

"Well, Miller Genuine Draft sponsors your man's, Rusty Wallace's, race team and makes the T-shirts and the hats and does those commercials on TV and has the big black-and-gold eighteen-wheelers at the track . . . why do you think they do that?"

"Because they can," he answered.

Of course, he was exactly right. Buying the race team, the stadium, the scoreboard, the blimp, the giant inflatable at the trade show—it's the corporate equivalent of buying a badge brand like a Porsche: "Because I can!"

And that never sold anything.

So perpetually ask the question: "How is spending this dollar going to win a vote?" And spend every dollar on momentum objectives and ask the tough question about how the next dollar is going to get you toward each of these goals.

Insurgents are often portrayed as visionaries and characterized as dreamers. What we find, however, is that truly successful revolutionaries practice cold realism. Indeed, their success depends upon their understanding the reality of the political landscape or marketplace better than the incumbent competition. And so the heart and soul of business insurgency comes down to a kind of ruthless practicality, even though business insurgency's strategies and tactics are very bold. Ask the tough question, to both yourself and those sitting next to you in every meeting: "How is spending this dollar going to win us a vote?"

Just do it. But do it by doing the doable. Just put one foot in front of the other. That, as Mao told us in his Little Red Book, is how the longest journey must start.

JUST DO IT

Do the doable. Winning starts with setting "momentum objectives."

- Teach your company to focus on achievable, but no-compromise, results—not the same old loosey-goosey objectives.
- Develop momentum objectives that teach the members of your team to be winners. Arrange them in reverse order of difficulty … get some wins.
- Create a spending discipline that is tied directly to strategy: "How is this dollar going to win a vote?"

Steps

- Choose your destiny. Define the future.
- Draw a doable road map to get there.
- Reject and punish excuses and office politics.
- Reward boldness and results.
- Define your customers', employees' and organization's future.

Exercises

- Write down in detail how you see your customers' lives 10 years into the future. What's it like there? How do these customers feel? How has your company or your brand helped make the customers' lives better?
- Write down what success looks like for you and your organization over the next two years and how this will benefit your customers. Define this in rigorous detail.
- Write a "conviction statement"—yourself or with a small, bold group of your company's all-stars:

  First, define your *conviction*: how you see the future; how it must be for you and your customers to succeed.

  Second, define the implied "therefore" in your conviction—the exact *mandate*; what must you do to bring about that view of the future?

  Third, define the specific, detailed, *focused actions* that will make this mandate successful.

- Define your goals in a sequence in order of difficulty. "Do the doable" means win the winnable first. Remember, hope is not a strategy. So brainstorm a set of doable, realistic goals. Write down 15 or 20 or more. Don't worry about how small they are. In fact, make sure they're doable. If they're not, put them on a separate list for later.

- Now turn your brainstorming into a list of momentum objectives by ordering the goals by difficulty: Which one is easiest? Second? Third? And so on. Tackle the easiest, most doable ones first to create momentum. The key is to start with the most achievable and move on from there.

- Assemble a "C team" and invest a day in planning an attack on your company, your brand, and its position in the market. Then invest another day in planning a counterattack. Consider using this counterattack before you have to, preemptively, against your competitor. As they say, "retaliate first."

- Draw a map of the competitive field and find a place where no one else is—find an open receiver and take what they give you. Check this competitive map weekly, even daily, and rethink and redraw it often—because it changes faster than you can imagine.

- Review all your tactics, including sponsorships, and assume that nothing is sacred. Now, ask yourself the hardest question about each: "How is this dollar going to win us a vote?" And if it isn't going to do that, get rid of it.

3

Move the Movable

"The problem with those votes is you can buy them—but they don't stay bought."

—TAMMANY HALL POLITICIAN

➤ *"Do the doable" focused on setting achievable objectives for your business. "Move the movable" focuses on creating a doable strategy—a strategy that achieves those objectives.*

➤ *Narrow your targets to the "voters" that you need to win and the "voters" you can move.*

➤ *Don't break your pick on the impossible.*

➤ *Don't focus on the undecided; buying their votes is too expensive.*

➤ *Learn the marketing strategies and tactics that move early adopters, the world's most powerful advertising medium.*

To succeed in an age of increasing competition and clutter, you've got to learn to be much more opportunistic and aggressive than ever before. No matter what your position in the marketplace may be, you've got to be scrapping like an underdog.

In politics, even the incumbent has to think and act this way. Fewer and fewer political races these days are blowouts. The orneriness of the voters, the even split of the electorate among Democrats, Republicans, and Independents, and the self-interest of the media in keeping the public tuned in keep candidates close into the last 2 weeks of almost any election. And, as we all learned in the 2000 presidential election, *every vote counts.* Today, this is true among any democratic constituency, including consumers, employees, corporate boards, and shareholders. So you've got to learn to fight for every vote you can get. And, in business, because you've got elections on a monthly, daily, or even hourly basis, every vote adds up.

WHY YOU MUST MOVE THE MOVABLE

You've also got to learn not to waste your energy and time fighting for votes you can't get. Political campaign strategy teaches you to be both opportunistic (make that desperate) and practical at the same time. You fight like hell, but only for the votes you can reasonably get (the point of "do the doable" in Chapter 2). This is why there's a corollary principle: "move the movable."

- "Do the doable" describes how to develop better objectives.
- "Move the movable" describes how to develop better strategy—the objectives are your destination; the strategy is your road map.

Developing a "move the movable" strategy starts with defining your market targets. Most companies today do a pretty good job of defining their market targets in terms of demographics or psychographics. You'll see the target defined in terms of age, race, gender, income, and geography and in terms of lifestyle, purchase activity, or aspirations. In the end, however, companies most often opt for mass communications, rationalizing that the spillover from their specific target "can't hurt and could help." Indeed, most companies go for "eyeballs"—forgetting that these eyeballs are attached to very different brains. These days, they'll tighten their focus somewhat with cable TV, the Web, and specialty magazines. And they'll spend everything they can afford in order to hit their desirable targets . . . and then some.

Politics, however, is more pragmatic. We segment the market in terms of *attitude*: How are they likely to vote and how likely are they to vote? Moreover, we don't select targets that are merely desirable—they must also be *movable*, and we have to be able to move them to vote the right way. Similarly, today it should be the same in business—because the best use of your marketing and sales resources and the best way to move an internal or stakeholder audience is to focus on attitude.

- *Our "do the doable" objectives have helped us identify the votes that we need to win.* But, among these constituents, who will vote? And who will influence these voters?

- *Our "move the movable" strategy focuses us on those who can be moved most efficiently.* And, true to the principles of "do the doable," we order our target priorities in terms of easiest first, followed by the progressively more difficult—all those who are necessary if we are to get to the 50.1 percent that gets the win.

Demographic and psychographic segmentations are useful. But we suggest that you impose attitudinal segmentation on top of these definitions. This segmentation should be used for any group, internal or external: employees, distributors, sales targets, current customers, investors, analysts, regulators, journalists, boards of directors, activists—*any* group. Attitudinal segmentation tells you where to place your resources in order to get the win. It focuses you not only on where to start your success, but also on where to start the momentum that will ensure that success.

This is what an attitudinal segmentation map looks like in politics:

HO SO UNDECIDED SOS HAS

Here's what each group represents.

HO = Hard Opposition

These people hate your candidate and the horse he rode in on, and they'll come out in a driving blizzard to vote against that candidate. You must write these people off. They are categorically ungettable. Of course, you don't ignore them completely; you must be aware of their effect on other voter groups. All this is obvious . . . maybe. But it's part of human nature, particularly among ambitious sales and marketing human beings, to include unwinnable targets in strategies— simply because they represent a challenge and because it makes macho PowerPoint presentation material to say that you plan to "climb the unclimbable."

- You're in a meeting, and you're getting significant pushback from somebody on the other side of the table. It's natural to want to confront the criticism. It's natural to want to win an argument. But it's pointless. Ignore the unmovable and concentrate on the movable. As you read on, you'll see how to do it.

When you try to do the undoable, you don't just waste resources; you waste energy, divert focus, demoralize yourself and your colleagues, and energize the enemy. Bad idea.

SO = Soft Opposition

These voters support the other candidate; in other words, they prefer your competitor's brand. But they're not loyalists. A slight drizzle on Election Day may keep them at home. In a political campaign, the objective is not to raise any issue that might activate the soft opposition to get off their butts and vote. You don't want to inflame them. You want the election to be a nonevent for them.

In consumer marketing, though, you have an infinite number of Election Days, and the soft opposition often has attractive long-term potential. But underline "long-term." This is exactly where *not* to start your campaign. These are the cynics, the doubters of your brand story. Remember the low credibility of broadcast television advertising. It's the hard opposition and soft opposition who drive it down there.

Think about the way you manage your own employees. When you're facing a critical issue or crisis, where do you start? You start where the wheels squeak the loudest. You focus your oilcan (with valuable oil in it and your valuable time attached to it) on lubricating these wheels to shut them up and seemingly win them over. In doing so, not only do you overspend critical resources, but you often set up an internal value system that assumes that all votes have to be bought for the same price—and, usually, these are very high-priced votes.

Undecided

A political campaign is generally run every 2, 4, or 6 years in the United States (but these campaigns are staggered in such a way that it seems that there's *always* one going on). In between elections, campaign organizations concentrate on amassing the vast resources and credibility that they'll need in order to run again successfully. During the campaign, all eyes are on Election Day and all minds are focused on what it will take to get 50.1 percent of the votes that day. Most often, this means moving a large block of undecided voters to pull your lever (or touch your spot on the CRT display, or, in Florida, fully detach your chad).

As any voter realizes, campaigns will do anything in order to move the undecided on Election Day. They'll try to buy the votes—with outright "Florida money," as it is called on the cold streets of a Philadelphia November, or with issues, trading favors that will be paid off in office. They'll run negative advertising at the last possible moment. They'll unleash rash charges against an opponent. They'll do *anything*. After all, they've got 2 or 4 or 6 years to try to live down the campaign's excesses. This, of course, gets expensive. And that's why campaigns spend every minute of the intervening years trying to bulldoze money into their now-empty coffers. It's also not very effective: Votes that are bought are loyal to the price paid, not to the candidate who did the paying. As that Tammany Hall saying goes: "The problem with those votes is you can buy them—but they don't *stay* bought."

You have to buy voters' loyalty over and over again. And the price usually goes up as the election gets closer. And, in the business world, if you've got a product in the market, you may have to win an election every year, every quarter, every day, or even several times a day. So if you're only *buying* votes (not attracting them), it gets a little pricey. Of course, this may seem obvious, but some of mass marketing's most accepted strategies and tactics actually require this. Indeed, most marketers realize that you essentially buy the first sale and sometimes several sales after that with the costs of development, distribution, and introductory marketing. *Price promotion is essentially buying votes.*

- This week your product is on special. Next week, the special is another competitor's product, and the week after that it's a store's private-label brand: In fact, this usually goes in order of market position—from biggest brand to next biggest brand to next biggest brand, and so on. And most competitors in most markets have an amazingly civil attitude toward price promotion: Don't step on a competitor's price promotion. "Why bother? Our offer might just get lost," they reason. The result is serial price promotions by various competitors. And the undecided in any marketplace—the "brand unaffiliated"—are moved … from one brand to the next and the next and the next.

This is probably the safest, most proven way to move consumers in any market. What's not to like about a special low price? Consumers, however, are not idiots (ignore the "I'm with Stupid" trucker hats for a moment). They learn from marketing. And so they buy serially as marketers promote serially—your brand, your competitor's brand, and the store brand . . . rinse and repeat. Price promotion has a very poor record of motivating repeat sales—and even when it does, the repeat sale may come in sequence after the repeat sales of competitive products.

Still, marketers keep on using price promotion because "it works." The problem is, *it works for everybody.* Unless you can develop the lowest price in the marketplace every day, you don't have real market differentiation. Retailers encourage marketers to use price promotion. In fact, they often demand it: "If you want to move product, you've got to price-promote."

And so you do it. But if they told you, "If you want to make some money, put your kidneys up for sale on eBay," would you do it? Nobody ever got rich selling his or her body parts to science. And nobody ever did or ever will get rich price promoting to the undecided.

Think about the incentives used for years by AT&T, MCI (WorldCom), and Sprint in those telemarketing calls timed for precisely the moment when you were putting the first forkful of meat loaf into your mouth. At one point, there were over 250,000 consumers who were moving between AT&T and MCI *on a weekly basis* in order to get the incentive first from one, then from the other. At MCI, they called them "revolvers," because that's exactly what they were doing. If this was a "loss leader" promotion, it managed to achieve the dubious result of leading directly to permanent losses. And these are the kinds of boneheaded marketing practices that the CFO had to try to make up for by microwaving the books a few years later.

Wal-Mart is one retailer that doesn't have price promotion. Wal-Mart has everyday low prices (EDLP) that are "constantly rolling back" (as the merchants in Little Rock are constantly rolling back their suppliers' prices). *The low-cost operator*—like Southwest in the airline business or Dell in computers—*doesn't have to have the lowest price at any given time,* because it's established its brands as having a low price all the time.

On a given day, American or Delta will dive down below Southwest's prices to create a "sale." And this buys a day's worth of loyalty. Southwest holds its loyal customer franchise by refusing to play the games the big airlines play with their passengers. And no frills means no B.S., either.

Moving the undecided is imperative. But buying the undecided is stupid. The trick is to get somebody else to move them for you on the cheap.

SOS = Soft Support

These are the voters who may like your candidate, but who cannot be counted on to come out and vote in even a light drizzle. These are the consumers who like your brand, but don't buy it often enough, don't buy enough of it, or aren't willing to pay a premium for it. These are the employees who support management's objectives, but won't speak up against any opposition to them.

They say that 80 percent of golf is putting. It's getting the damned ball into the hole. Similarly, 80 percent of elections is getting the soft support to move toward hard support—activating them and getting them to vote. It's the same thing in marketing. Moving the soft support is the *whole deal.* Why? There are three reasons:

1. *The soft support is easier and cheaper to move than the undecided.* They're essentially on the threshold of support—on the lip of the cup. And the campaign manager's or marketer's job is to move them just that little bit . . . to give them just a little push. They may need more and more personally relevant reasons to buy. They may need more reasons to come back more often and buy more. And they may need more reasons that support your product's price. One of the oldest clichés of customer relationship management is the oft-proven fact that current customers are six times cheaper to sell than noncustomers. You're already in their consideration set; in fact, you're somewhere between

the on-deck circle and up to bat. All that's needed is the right push.

2. *You don't have to compromise your value system to move soft support.* Basically, soft supporters are attracted by your core values, which form your core political message. They simply need added emphasis on key aspects of your message. On the other hand, reaching out to elements of the undecided (or, God forbid, the soft opposition) often forces you to skate out beyond the thick, safe ice of your core beliefs and onto the thin ice of compromise—and often beyond that to the tepid water of self-contradiction. This is what destroys the faith of the faithful—this contradiction of your core principles breaks the covenant with your best customers and best employees. For the undecided—the people with their arms folded across their chests at your sales pitch meeting—you have to keep providing a better offer. And, as you do, you move further and further away from your core value proposition. Eventually you desert it altogether.

Consider, for example, the lengths to which Delta, United, and American Airlines go to convince the guy with the backpack and roaring BO to sit in that otherwise empty seat next to their full-fare passenger. Their soft support is full-fare business flyers. In a hyperbole of the old "20-80" rule, which says that in most businesses, 20 percent of the customers account for 80 percent of the sales (it's called Parado's curve, by the way), for the major airlines, usually under 10 percent of their flyers account for over 80 percent of revenues. Guess which 10 percent? *Hint:* It's not the backpacker sitting next to you with the "ZZZZZZZ-SMMMMMM-ZZZZZZ-SMMMMM-BUHHHHH" leaking through the earphones of his CD player, undoubtedly playing music he downloaded for free onto his MP3 player.

It's this compromise of the airlines' basic value proposition that turns their soft support into soft opposition, looking for any alternative to their hub airline this side of Greyhound. Think about it: Southwest, Jet Blue, Midwest Express, and AirTran have all established their brands as the anti–Delta-United-American airlines, the opposite of the market incumbents. And so your value system as a company must be baked into your basic selling proposition: *In return for X, you get Y-plus.* Compromising on that risks losing your best customers and prospects, as well as your best employees. Can you honestly say you're getting the maximum share of wallet from your own customers? If not, don't start trolling for new ones yet.

3. *The movement of soft support to hard support creates true market momentum.* It creates viral marketing—"buzz" is what it was called in the dot-coms' heyday. And it creates demonstrative testimony of your value proposition. Having spent many years helping breweries improve their marketing strategies, one truism shines through the mountains of market research: *What sells beer is selling beer.*

   In the beer business, it's something called "bar call." If beer drinkers see other beer drinkers ordering, enjoying, and then reordering your company's beer, you've got the world's most potent sales tool plugged in and humming. When consumers are calling out your brand name, it's far more effective than when you're calling it out to them. The ubiquitous beer ads blaring from the multiple TV monitors in sports bars these days sell a hell of a lot less beer than do the young beer drinkers who watch them. And one critically important segment of these beer drinkers, early adopters, sells more than all the others. This segment probably constitutes the most powerful advertising medium on earth.

Thus, moving the soft support toward harder support—so that they buy more, more often—means creating marketing momentum that communicates not only to consumers, but to retailers, distributors, investors, and on and on. As we've said before, traditional broadcast advertising has a low credibility, and it also has more and more difficulty reaching Y-Generation males. But word of mouth, by contrast, has very high credibility. What you hear and see among your friends, neighbors, and coworkers drives consideration, sampling, trial, and retrial.

And this effect of market momentum extends beyond the soft support. We've talked about how expensive it is to move the undecided. Today, the most efficient and effective way to move these undecided is by creating movement of the soft support. Obviously, the uncommitted in any market come in all shades. But those who are closer to soft support move first, and there is, indeed, a tipping point—when more and more see, hear, and feel more and more demonstrating their choice in a marketplace. When that avalanche happens, you get buried in money.

Now, and for many years to come, this will be the most important effort in Iraq and in much of the Muslim world—moving the soft support to at least *harder* support. This doesn't mean moving them to harder support of the United States and U.S. policy. That's undoable. Rather, it means moving them toward their own self-interest, toward harder support for the things that the fanatical Islamists oppose: freedom, progress, commerce, individual and artistic expression, equal rights for women, and human rights in general. It means moving musicians and playwrights and journalists and academics and athletes and fashionistas and novelists and filmmakers and dancers and political activists toward their own self-interests.

HAS = Hard Support

God bless the loyal customers. They are any company's lifeblood. But there simply aren't enough of them for most companies. These are the people paying $75,000-plus for their fifth or sixth Mercedes. They're the ones paying $4.96 for their third Vente latte of the day at Starbucks. They're the ones still paying two bucks for 10 ounces of Red Bull—roughly the price of a glass of Chanel No. 5—when that can is displayed shoulder-to-shoulder with Red Bull wannabes at something like half the price.

This is not to say, however, that the cost of these sales is zero—in fact, these brands have developed this hard support the old-fashioned way, through product experience. That's the loudest and longest-lasting communication of brand for *any* product or service. Build a better one and the hard support will keep on beating that same path to your door. For good reason, in business or in politics, you do anything you can to hold the hard support. And you do whatever you can to activate them to help you sell more by helping to move the soft support.

Several years ago, a debate raged in *Ad Age* over the uncovered fact that the TV viewers who were most likely to be paying attention to last night's Ford commercial were actually people who had bought a new Ford within the past 3 weeks. "What a waste of money!" the critics blathered.

But it's not so.

Think about it: What happens within the first 3 weeks after you park a new Ford in your driveway or company parking lot? You get dozens of friends and associates asking, "How do you like your new car?"

Supplying these people with more reinforcement and even more facts to sell is very good business—remember, this is the most effective advertising medium there is; these are your most productive salespeople. But, importantly, there are lots of ways of doing that without buying TV commercials.

In fact, the hard support can also help you develop the strategies that will move soft supporters. We call these "usage strategies," since it is usage that creates loyalty. If increased usage of your product doesn't create greater loyalty to the brand, then you've got a significant product problem. Moreover, remember that the most important brand communication is the product experience—something that most ad agencies don't take into account until they're presented with crappy sales results.

- *First, we do "loyal voter research."* We target the hard support with this research in order to understand how they define the product and product experience. (Most often, by the way, we've found that their definition of the product's meaning and benefits is different from that of the brand's managers.) And this hard support definition obviously drives greater usage among certain users. Are the needs of this group different from those of soft supporters? Chances are, their needs are not unique—but these "loyal voters" or hard supporters have found a way to use or think about your product or service that helps satisfy their needs uniquely.

  Too often, companies shape product development and refinement around the needs and wants of the undecided or even the soft opposition critics. Their goal in doing this is to create a more broadly appealing product. But we'll take deeper appeal over broader appeal any day. That's where the margins live. And broadening this deeper appeal profitably is easier than creating broad, but thin, appeal in the first place. Again and again, you can count on the viral communications of satisfied customers and the momentum of their purchasing and usage behavior in the marketplace to help pull the product out over larger geography.

  For example, the elephant's graveyard of the fast-food business is filled with chains that tried to expand a thin business concept too broadly. When you look at the Starbucks' same-store sales, you realize that its deep concept has been pulled across the country—indeed, now across the world—by its hard support brand meaning.

- *Once you understand the product in the minds of your hard support, you can test their personalized brand positioning.* You can test the way hard supporters define the brand's benefits and differentiation and the ways in which they use the product or service among soft supporters. Does this help convince the soft supporters to come back more often and buy more—or pay more?

In other words, does this hard support positioning help create greater usage among soft supporters? Usage means trial, reconsideration, and repurchase. And when soft supporters increase their usage of any product or service, the activity has a seismic effect on the marketplace.

In 2003, for example, McDonald's/USA began attracting about a million "new" customers a month into its U.S. restaurants and drive-through lanes. But, of course, these customers weren't truly new—they were soft supporters whose usage had fallen away occasion by occasion over the previous several years. And the benefits that had once drawn them to McDonald's more often had been either lost or "seen" in the marketplace by other fast-food players. So McDonald's began a new series of tactics and actions:

- Salads with Paul Newman's organic dressings didn't exactly bring moms back to McDonald's. But it brought their purchases back. They'd been coming through to purchase Happy Meals for their kids, but not purchasing for themselves.

- Now that they had found an appealing menu item for themselves, moms convinced more of their teenage children to come along. Big Mac sales went up by 40 to 50 percent after the introduction of the Newman salads.

- And McDonald's has kept up the pace of adding relevant and differentiated benefits focused on the needs and wants of its hard support: McGriddles breakfast sandwiches, healthier treats for Happy Meals, a "healthy Happy Meal" for adults, and all-white-meat McNuggets.

In fact, in order to build its business in the United States efficiently and effectively, McDonald's doesn't need to build a single new restaurant. And it doesn't really have to attract a single new customer. It simply has to convince current customers to come back more often and buy more. And so the hard supporters' perceptions and attitudes provide very useful guidelines for McDonald's U.S. President Mike Roberts and his leadership team.

Today, then, McDonald's is getting the basics better, from burgers and fries to broadcast advertising. Still, by far, the most effective ad media are the restaurants (walls, menu boards, posters, tray-liners, bags, and cups), the people (the service and attitude of the managers and crews), the drive-through lanes, and satisfied customers.

TAKE OUT A PENCIL AND PAPER

Of course, it's best to do market research to create this attitudinal segmentation among market targets. And we are strong advocates of such research: We don't let our clients leave home without it. But we've found, too, that our clients often can do a good job of developing this segmentation informally, particularly with internal or small client audiences.

So line up the five categories—hard opposition, soft opposition, undecided, soft support, and hard support—and begin to drop people (or customers) into each bucket based solely on your perception of their attitude toward your company and brand. We'll bet the longest list will be in the soft support category. Unless you've encountered a significant crisis of faith, there isn't likely to be any hard opposition among your customer franchise—those people will have departed long ago. But, even in the best of times, you'll identify a few that can be categorized as soft opposition. Whether they're among your employees or your customer franchise, these are the ones you probably call the "squeaky wheels." And, too often, they get the largest share of your mind and resources. It's the soft support, like Nixon's "Silent Majority," who demand little, but promise so much.

Now, how can you develop a strategy to realize this promise and move soft support to hard support? What will it take to convince these people to buy more, buy more often, or pay more? What's the doable strategy—the one that will gain you ground the most easily? This is not about creating an event, but a process. You must add reasons why on top of reasons why. You must remind these people constantly of the benefits you provide them—not your product or service attributes—and you must remind them constantly of how you do that uniquely. Later, in Chapter 6, we'll teach you a formula for developing long-term customer satisfaction, which, in essence, means constantly giving the soft support reasons to move to hard support.

Again and again, it's your current customers who provide the most powerful and cost-effective marketing force to attract new customers. But it's up to you to activate them. It's up to you to activate the hard support to recommend your brand to others.

TRANSFER OWNERSHIP

When it comes to moving soft support employees, there is an important principle: transfer of ownership. The point is that people will fight harder for something that they own. If a strategy is imposed upon them, they will do their job. But if a strategy is developed *with* them and if they feel that they *own* it, they'll do their job a lot better. Now it's personal.

Having developed our work principles in domestic and international politics, we've learned "up close and personal" the power of democracy. Democracy works. It unites people under a common purpose. Democracy is good. More democracy is better. Fluid democracy is best.

That's true in any government or institution—democracy is dialogue, and the better the conversation, the better things go for the government or institution. Developing action means developing consensus for it through a democratic dialogue.

Most companies have *some* democracy. And many managers brag that a process that they're in charge of is *not* going to be democratic. They mean to say that they're not going to get pushed around. Being democratic is not about getting pushed around, nor is it about pushing other people around. Leading in a democracy means listening and allowing those whom you lead to shape your strategy for action, then pursuing this action with the constituents' approval. According to most of the business books on shelves near this one, this is the best way of leading a company, not just a country.

Transfer of ownership is part of this:

1. You develop a rough-draft strategy.

2. You "walk" this strategy around your group. As you hear comments, you make refinements or course corrections. Yes, you sell, but, yes, you also listen.

3. You expand the "walk" outward to your distribution system or among market parties or other key stakeholder groups.

4. As you continue to develop the strategy through market research or other tests, you incorporate the refinements that have been suggested by your group and others.

5. When you have finalized the strategy, you walk it around again. As you do so, you make it very clear how each stakeholder's suggestions have been incorporated.

In this process, you've transferred ownership of your strategy. And this can also be done with your consumer franchise. You can and should communicate to them: *"We hear you."* Incorporate this message into any change in operations, product, or service/support.

This was done on an epic scale by the leaders of The Coca-Cola Company, particularly Coke President Don Keough, during the so-called New Coke fiasco in the 1980s. With the return of "Classic Coke" 77 days after the introduction of "New Coke," Keough, in fact, went on national television to say, "We were wrong, but we listened to you."

Keough transferred ownership of the return of "Classic Coca-Cola" to consumers. And the result wasn't just a return of the core hard support to the brand—in fact, there was a tidal wave of soft supporters moving to hard support. In the end, The Coca-Cola Company received a boost of something on the order of three or four positive share points on Pepsi, at about $500 million per share point.

WIN EARLY ADOPTERS—AND WIN IT ALL

The first consumers of many new products are called "early adopters." They are the most consumerist of all consumers. They are the most sensitive to marketing communications. They're very self-confident in making marketplace decisions. And they self-select—in other words, you don't have to ask them to look for new products, because they do so every time they shop.

Most important, these early adopters strongly influence other consumers. Early adopters lead others to new products through their demonstrated behavior in the marketplace and their word-of-mouth advertising of new concepts. Early adopters provide the "point of the wedge" of greater consumer support. And early adopters are willing to pay a premium to try a new product or idea.

Unfortunately, early adopters are notoriously disloyal. They're like serial philanderers—they're constantly trolling for something new and exciting. While they are your customers, they are hard supporters. And, to be sure, holding early adopters is not absolutely impossible. *But you cannot possibly prevent them from trying other new ideas as they come along.* In fact, the best you can do to hold these early adopters is to maintain and upgrade or refresh the relevant and differentiated benefits that brought them to your product in the first place.

Early adopters still stand in line at Starbucks. The reason we can say this with confidence is that Starbucks maintains its early adopter price structure. The early adoption phase of any new product is almost always the highest-margin volume you'll ever get (though not necessarily the most profitable, because of the high costs of introducing a new product through mass marketing). And when you see a product begin to price-promote, it's almost surely a sign that the product has begun to lose its hold on early adopters.

In understanding that these are the universe's most consumerist consumers and the most marketing-sensitive marketing targets, you should also understand that they are just about the most cynical consumers around. These early adopters have seen it all, paid attention to it all, and tried it all. So they will not be fooled twice. And they view mass advertising with great suspicion, not only because they question its credibility, but because they assume that mass-marketed products are being adopted by the masses—and the early adopters don't *ever* want to be part of the masses.

For example, in market research for Coca-Cola a few years ago, teens talked about an idea becoming massively popular as the "mall phase." And once they saw something on a T-shirt displayed in a mall kiosk, they knew that it was over as a cool thing.

Early adopters pay attention to mass advertising, but it tends to have the opposite of the intended effect on them—it pushes them away in droves.

So what kind of marketing works with early adopters? First and foremost, "It's the Product, Stupid."

Product effect and integrity are paramount with early adopters. The truth is, *product quality, integrity, and credibility are more important today with all consumers than at any time since the beginning of mass marketing, more than 50 years ago.* Consumers want to know more about products than ever before. They read labels. They read articles. They read web sites and enter chat rooms. They listen to other consumers. And they are one very tough audience for marketing B.S. In the end, consumers today will turn on a product or service with a vengeance if it fails to do what was promised in its marketing communications.

But today, packaged goods marketing is lagging in response to this phenomenon. Most new products are clones of old products, or provide only a shade of difference. And these new ideas are usually dressed up to look like real change. They may even get trial from early adopters—but soon they'll be dropped like a bad habit. That's why early adopters are rooting around the edges of big-brand shelf space for the truly new ideas.

- *Since early adopters are looking for new ideas, rule number one in developing more effective marketing for them is developing more truly new ideas.* Swing for the fences in product development. And bench any new idea that doesn't provide a real, meaningful difference.

- *For most of the insurgent new brands in the bottom tier of today's marketplaces, distribution* is *marketing.* These brands must be found by early adopters—because they can't afford to call on early adopters with advertising (and anyway, it wouldn't be effective if they did). Moreover, these new insurgent brands in the bottom tier must be found in the right places. New brands develop associative imagery through the company they keep: If you're introduced in a cool venue, you become more cool. And early adopters like to feel a sense of discovery and ownership of the channel and even of the store placement in which they discover a brand.

   For example, early adopters discovered Red Bull energy drinks in liquor stores and at dance club bars. These aren't the typical venues for soft drink introductions. But this distribution helped set Red Bull apart and at the same time helped establish its badass reputation for potency.

   USA Today established itself as a national newspaper by free distribution in hotels and airports. Gannett wanted to prove the concept on people who were time-stressed and information-hungry.

- *Package design is important in developing differentiation on the shelf.* Remember, a lot of the insurgent ideas are on the market's "bottom-est" shelf. They have to stand out. But these insurgent ideas are at least willing to diverge, whereas the big-brand packages all converge. In every single marketplace, from petroleum to pet food, it's the insurgents who have driven new packaging concepts that have later been adopted by the established brands. Innovate. As the late Roberto Goizueta of Coca-Cola said, "Be different or be damned!"

- *Early adopters read labels—more than all other consumer groups do these days.* As we'll discuss further in Chapter 7, today's store aisles have become the "hot zone" of marketing in every retail category, because of time stress and marketing clutter. People feel very confident about making choices in the store, often on impulse. They're superinformed. And early adopters hunt for new ideas in a learning mode. They're looking for differences in materials and ingredients, even in place of manufacture.

- *Merchandising works.* Odwalla, for example, developed its own refrigerated display cases to emphasize its natural qualities. And Starbucks established a unique retail space for something that used to be at the end of the deli line. 7-Eleven established the convenience store with an emphasis on the basics for young males—milk, soda, beer, and cigarettes. And Nike used Niketown to create a fountain of brand meaning in the midst of other retail distributors.

- *Once you have established distribution in the "cool" places, you can and must move to wider distribution.* If you've got a truly new idea, you may want to advertise it—because mass marketing does its best job in announcing truly new news in the marketplace. But ultimately, the key is to focus on adding communications close to the product that articulate new ideas, new forms, new packaging, new materials, new placement, new events, new promotions, and new, hyper-local PR. This, for example, is what Red Bull did with dance club events and early sponsorship of extreme sports events locally.

All this constitutes early adopter marketing. A brand like Starbucks has never stopped its early adopter marketing strategies and tactics, even after a decade of success. And this, indeed, may account for the fact that Starbucks still commands early adopter pricing.

Moving the movable means focusing on these early adopters—their needs and wants. When the great Mickey Drexler was truly "on his game" with Gap, he was developing his product and merchandising in line with the attention span and perceptions of his most loyal customers. That meant changing things often. While his relevant competition—at the time, big department stores—was changing only on a seasonal basis, Mickey knew that his most important customers would be passing by the stores and looking for new news on a *weekly* basis.

It's been pointed out to us that there is an importance to our orthodoxy, and so *you must follow every step to get an insurgent strategy right.* We agree. It's true that you can't cut corners: To achieve your "do the doable" objectives, you must adopt "move the movable" strategies. The simple fact is that this stuff works. Don't dabble—just do it.

JUST DO IT

Move the movable. Develop an insurgent strategy and start getting revolutionary results.

- "Do the doable" focused on setting achievable objectives for your business. "Move the movable" focuses on creating a doable strategy—a strategy that achieves those objectives.
- Narrow your targets to the "voters" that you need to win and can move.
- Don't break your pick on the impossible.
- Don't focus on the undecided; buying their votes is too expensive.
- Activate the world's most powerful advertising medium—early adopters.

Steps

- Develop doable business objectives.
- Target your efforts internally or externally by attitude.
- Focus on the voters you need in order to win the election.
- Forget the undecided—get others to move them.
- Drive word of mouth and viral marketing tactics.
- Give your early adopters almost anything they want.

Exercises

- Draw a continuum and put your customers, employees, or audiences in separate categories based on their support and loyalty:

  Hard opposition

  Soft opposition

  Undecided

  Soft support

  Hard support

- Consider conducting "loyal voter" research to understand better what exactly your hard support sees in you. Get them to say why exactly they love you.

- Organize by priority new news that will move these "loyal voters"—hard supporters and soft supporters—toward your product, service, or offering.

- Internally, write a rough-draft strategy including your objectives, overall strategic imperatives, key themes and messages, tactics, and organization.

- Walk your rough draft around your group. Get comments. Promote dialogue. Listen. And keep improving it.

- Now, assign a team to walk this improved strategy around your larger system. Keep getting it better and keep selling it in. Keep communicating: "I want to hear from you. I want you to own this strategy." Transfer ownership of your strategy to others—others in your group or in your company or distribution system, and among your customers.

- Treat your early adopters like gold—because they are. Use research to ask them how you can keep delivering relevance and differentiation. More and more. Better and better. More new ideas. Finally, get them to tell you where exactly they are day to day and how best to communicate with them—and where they will soon be going and listening to you.

4

Play Offense

"In any form of combat, whoever goes on the offense first wins."

—Bill Clinton

➤ *Ride ahead of today's waves of change.*

➤ *Define yourself—before your opponent defines you.*

➤ *Get scared. And stay scared.*

➤ *Don't play not to lose—play to win.*

➤ *When in doubt, play offense.*

The insurgent campaign has a bias for action. That's because the insurgent has a commanding need for change. The incumbent is trying to maintain stability—the status quo is exactly what the incumbent wants. If the insurgent is going to be successful, she or he must disrupt that stability. The insurgent must change the political dialogue if she or he is going to win.

To win, *the insurgent must constantly take the battle to the incumbent*: The insurgent must play offense. For any week, day, or hour of the campaign that the insurgent is on the defensive, that insurgent is losing ground—the incumbent is in control.

An example that you'll see again and again in the 2004 national, statewide, and local political campaigns is an insurgent's demand for a debate. It's not just that the insurgent wants to pit his or her policies and personality against the incumbent's. The insurgent's primary objective is to be placed on the same stage as the incumbent—literally on the same level. That defines the campaign as a horse race, and that, in itself, is a victory for the insurgent.

A bias for action is just as important in business as it is in politics. But that attitude has all but evaporated in the post–9/11 business environment. To be fair, the period after 9/11 was the perfect storm for American corporations: The Internet bubble had burst, the economy had already slipped into recession, and the terrorist attacks created an atmosphere of insecurity that virtually paralyzed our nation. British Prime Minister Tony Blair summed up the situation very well: "A kaleidoscope has been shaken."

This perfect storm of negative effects became the perfect excuse for inaction within the executive offices of our nation's corporations. Inside these offices, people were not taking bold action, not reinventing, not hiring . . . in fact, many had assumed the fetal position under their impressive corporate desks. Ingenious innovator Doug Hall, founder of the concept development oasis Eureka! Ranch in Cincinnati, has found in his research that U.S. business leaders have less courage to act and less optimism today than at any point in recent history.

Finally, though, a few companies and their leaders have begun to move. Predictably, it's the insurgents who have moved first. Consider the U.S. airline industry. The major airlines are still struggling, using every defensive tactic to maintain stability: Chapter 11 protection, massive layoffs, calls for employee sacrifice and government bailouts, and, of course, continual chipping away at passenger comfort and service. Meanwhile, the insurgents are thriving: Jet Blue, AirTran, and Southwest. "What problems?" they ask.

Hiding behind the recession was fundamental market disruption: The middle market has disappeared or is disappearing in most, if not all, categories. Now the market is configured with a top tier of massive brands and a bottom tier of so-called niche customized and personalized brands. It's a classic configuration of incumbents versus insurgents. And it's the insurgents who are on the march. Nearly every new idea is coming from that bottom tier these days.

Today, whether you are at the top of the market or the bottom, you have the choice of playing defense like an incumbent or playing offense like an insurgent. But is that really a choice? We want to convince you to play offense. Whether you're number one or number fifty in your market, you can choose to play offense, to develop an insurgent culture, to take the battle to the market. In that battle, the consumer is always the winner, as the pace of change and innovation is increased while market offers are raised and seen and raised again. As a result, companies today have an unprecedented opportunity—maybe it's what a colleague once described as "an insurmountable opportunity"—to reconceptualize their business around new opportunities, to change their marketplace dialogue, to exploit new information-age forces, and to revitalize the fundamentals of their company.

We live in a new environment since September 11, 2001. We call it the "reset environment." It's a time when individuals at every level of every business or consumer market are reconsidering every one of their relationships (personal, institutional, or brand) from a zero base. And in this time of political instability and challenge for the United States, Secretary of State Colin Powell defined a key principle of the Bush Doctrine shortly before our attack on the Taliban thugs' government in Afghanistan: "Never underestimate the cost of inaction."

With change coming more quickly than ever, consider the cost of ignoring it, resisting it, or trying to defend against it. That cost is incalculable in terms of loss of control, loss of morale and conviction, loss of share, and loss of your future.

Furthermore, it's not just market competition that threatens today—hyperaggressive media, emboldened activists, opportunistic litigators, politically motivated regulators, and international terrorists also offer major challenges. So, in this reset environment, depending on the advantages of market leadership represents a dangerous complacency. Learning to think, plan, and act like an insurgent is the only way to survive and thrive. If you're playing defense, you're playing by somebody else's rules, on somebody else's home field. That's playing to keep from losing, not playing to win.

It's not enough to make one bold move in the marketplace. Playing offense is about constant movement forward—a constant attack. That means that *you have to instill an insurgent spirit in your company culture.* To show you how to do that, we'll draw on many of the principles that are repeated throughout this book.

1. Define success—define the enemy.
2. Represent choice and change.
3. Set an example of bold initiative.
4. Create a bias for action.
5. Take what they give you.
6. Don't meet armies with armies.
7. Take control of the dialogue and never let go.
8. Sustain the attack.
9. Celebrate every win.
10. Never act like the incumbent.

DEFINE SUCCESS—DEFINE THE ENEMY

Your people can't play to win if they don't understand the stakes of the game. What does winning mean? You should define it in three ways:

- First, and most importantly, *what will winning mean for your customers?* How will it make their lives better?

- Second, *what will winning mean for the company and all its stakeholders?*

- Third, *what will winning mean for the individual employee?*

In Chapter 2, we recommended developing a number of achievable goals on the road to ultimate victory. Define the ultimate goal, and define the steps that will get you there—5 yards at a time. Don't let any objective be too daunting. Arrange your actions in order of the difficulty of the challenge, then take on the least difficult first and establish momentum by getting a few easy wins. Define success in terms of a victory of action over inaction and decisiveness over timidity.

One great way to sharpen your definition of victory and success is to find an enemy. Think, for example, of what The Coca-Cola Company's late chairman, Roberto Goizueta, said: "Without an enemy, there can be no war."

Several years ago, we conducted a study for South Korean President-elect Kim Dae Jung, a long-term client, who was about to take office amidst his country's worst financial crisis since the Korean War. We wanted to identify those leaders who were most successful over their first 100 days—who began their terms in office with the best running start and ultimately used this great beginning to define a positive historical legacy.

We looked hard for examples. Clinton suffered mishaps in his dealings with the issue of gays in the military and in a string of nomination disasters. Other leaders wasted their first 100 days and never regained critical momentum in defining themselves and their legacies.

So we selected the best three: President Franklin Roosevelt, British Prime Minister Margaret Thatcher, and President Ronald Reagan. All three enjoyed relatively high levels of popularity following their first 100 days in office. All three cemented their places in history from extraordinarily strong beginnings. And all three defined themselves and, in many ways, controlled the entire process of this definition. For example, all three leaders:

- Seized strategic and aggressive control of the dialogue from the beginning.

- Focused, disciplined, and defined themselves by a series of actions that communicated optimism and energetic leadership for the future.

- Aimed at an "enemy" in order to sharpen their own definition of themselves, the causes for which they stood, and their ultimate success.

For Roosevelt, the enemy was a group of "uncaring, mindless bureaucrats." For Thatcher, it was "socialist overspenders." For Reagan, it was supporters of "big government." These leaders energized their own definition of themselves and of success by defining the people they were against.

In business, consider the clarity an insurgent brings to a marketplace competition by defining itself against a big, bloated, bureaucracy-loving incumbent—against a marketplace "enemy." Indeed, even a great company like Microsoft can lose its focus until it finds such an enemy. For example, in 1994, the enemy was Novell. In 1995 and 1996, it was Netscape. In 1997 and 1998, it was Sun. And today, it's Linux and the so-called open systems.

So if you want to instill a winning culture in your company, your people need an opponent on which to focus. Importantly, this is not about blind hatred, but rather about cool competition. Don't overestimate or underestimate your opponent's strengths, and never "dis" your opponent: Teach your people to respect the competitor and learn from its strengths, but to exploit its weaknesses. Often, defining the enemy is easy—if you're not number one in the marketplace. You may want to take on the leader or the next competitor up the ladder. But don't diffuse your organization's focus by taking on everybody at once—or by making the more usual mistake of claiming, "We don't really have competition for what we do."

Often, the best enemy to define is a problem that consumers face in the marketplace. It may be a problem that innovation will solve; it may be a problem that consumer education will solve; it may be a problem created by one or two big players' marketplace domination . . . stagnation of choice. Microsoft's 1980s mission—"a computer on every desk and in every home"—was about the information revolution's march of progress and a conviction that this revolution would make all people's lives better.

REPRESENT CHOICE AND CHANGE

Americans inherently resent a monopoly. And they suspect bigness. The entire raison d'être for the Linux operating system is its position as the "anti-Microsoft," the anti-bigness candidate in the operating system marketplace. Even liberal Democrats claim to be against "big government" today.

Limited choice and stagnation of innovation characterize monopolized markets. Customers of every American industry sector inherently mistrust "bigness leaders." And so the burden of proof is always on the market dominator to show that it, too, can "try harder."

Whether you lead the market or not, in order to instill an insurgent culture, you must make your brands and your company represent choice and change in the marketplace. As we've said again and again, incumbents hate choice (like the Islamist theocrats who throttle the democratic process in the Middle East, they say, "Who needs choice?") and fear change. They want a stable state. And your job is to destabilize and disrupt. Force choice. And force change. Make everything about your brands represent change and refreshment of the incumbent's marketplace offer. Build your brand around the concept of change and choice in five key dimensions that lead you to your brand destination and to success:

- *Activated presence.* Incumbents dominate by the force of their mass. They are ubiquitous. Insurgents, by contrast, gain awareness and acceptability in a very different way—by creating an activated presence, the demonstrative usage of their product by early adopters, word of mouth and other forms of viral communications, and a sense of momentum as they expand distribution.

- *Relevant benefits.* The consumer benefits of the incumbent's products have probably been around the market long past their "freshness date." They've become mere table stakes in the market competition. And so when you define the benefits for your product or service, you must understand consumer needs better than the incumbent does. Because of the incumbent's reluctance to change, chances are that it is falling behind in terms of meeting consumers' perceived needs. Or the incumbent may be aware of the need for updating its benefits, but be afraid of disrupting its own value proposition. And, invariably, this provides a natural opening, a natural market gap for you to fill with more clear and present benefits.

- *Competitive differentiation.* Of course, you know that value is created by differentiation—because value is created by scarcity. Today, though, most markets are dominated by the undifferentiated and implicit brand positioning "me, too!" Most companies are very content to accept the category-defined benefits of usage (these are the market rules as written by the incumbent in most cases). But you must differentiate if you want to disrupt your marketplace's status quo. This differentiation, moreover, must be clearly apparent—in fact, the more obscure you are, the louder these differences must scream. Look around your own favorite supermarket—where are the changes in formulation, packaging, and placement coming from? In almost every case it's the smaller, insurgent brands. It's that bottom tier of the market.

- *Brand credibility.* Every brand provides an implicit promise. And credibility is built by delivering on that promise time after time. In fact, credibility is created most successfully by the formula we detail in Chapter 6, "Forget Reality: Perceptions Rule." Define expectations in advance, overdeliver on those expectations, and constantly remind your customers what you do for them uniquely. In other words, underpromise and overdeliver. You can almost surely contrast this attitude to the "manifest destiny" of the incumbent—who often feels that it owns the market and all the consumers in it. Almost always, this attitude is communicated loudly in the details of the incumbent's operations and actions.

- *Change imagery.* Every brand has a set of images and symbols associated with it. Make sure that yours clearly represent change and refreshment. Create a new look; break the marketplace rules. For years, it was assumed that an imported beer should come in a green bottle, just like the leader Heineken. But the number-one import in the United States today is Corona in its distinctive—in Mexico it's considered just plain cheap—clear bottle. Change the rules in every detail (learn more about this in Chapter 7, "Herd the Details").

SET AN EXAMPLE OF BOLD INITIATIVE

Creating an insurgent culture depends upon change leadership at the top of the company. When you are the boss, your people will most often listen to what you say, but they will almost always do what you do. Lead by example. First, set the example of taking action—*do something!* Today, with so many executives still trying to avoid making mistakes, taking action creates leadership differentiation. Do something big and bold. And impress upon your organization or team that you all face a simple and demanding choice: *change or be changed.* You can play by the other guy's rules or set the rules yourself. Follow the example of these change leaders:

- *The* Washington Post*'s Katharine Graham.* Following the suicide of her husband in 1963, Graham inherited an undistinguished regional newspaper and admits simply in her memoirs, "I was terrified."

In 1971, CEO Graham faced a critical decision: Should she publish a leaked Defense Department study detailing Vietnam War deceptions, called the Pentagon Papers? Either way, the consequences of her decision might put the entire company at risk. Graham concluded, however, that *not* printing the Pentagon Papers would contradict the company's very soul and purpose. She published—and started a trajectory that helped transform modern U.S. journalism. Soon thereafter, Graham was making tough and correct calls on covering the Watergate scandal and managing a 1976 strike. And the *Post* went on both to Supreme Court vindication over its decision to publish the Pentagon Papers and to become one of the top 50 IPOs over the past 25 years.

- *Johnson & Johnson's James Burke.* Burke is famous for his brilliant handling of the 1982 Tylenol recall after the product was sabotaged with cyanide. But, as author Jim Collins argues, "Burke's real defining moment occurred 3 years before, when he pulled 20 key executives into a room and thumped his finger on a copy of the J&J credo. Penned 36 years earlier by R. W. Johnson Jr., it laid out the 'We hold these truths to be self-evident' of the Johnson & Johnson Co., among them a higher duty to 'mothers and all others who use our products.'"

In fact, Burke believed that his executives had lost touch with the company's vision. According to Joseph Badaracco and Richard Ellsworth in *Leadership and the Quest for Integrity*, Burke said: "Here's the credo. If we're not going to live by it, let's tear it off the wall." Stunned executives spent hours debating and recommitting to the document—a decision that brought the credo alive, changed the internal culture, and made it almost easy to decide to pull the entire national inventory of Tylenol in 1982, at a cost of $100 million in earnings.

Burke's courageous leadership set in motion years of competitive and financial success for the company.

- *Wal-Mart's Sam Walton.* Walton built and led the company with an unusual mix of both promotional and operational talent. Walton's vision: to make better things ever more affordable to people of lesser means.

  Walton launched the superstore empire on an amazing trajectory of success by setting goalposts out beyond the immediately achievable. His initial goal: grow annual sales from less than $30 billion to $125 billion by 2000.

  Ultimately, under the steady stewardship of Walton's personally chosen successor, David Glass, the company not only changed the way America shops, but hit an amazing $165 billion in annual sales in 2000—8 years after Walton's own death.

  Walton practiced the principle of "take what they give you." He concentrated his construction of Wal-Mart stores in the rural areas that big department stores and discounters had ignored. He moved away from suburban malls to stand-alone stores outside smaller cities and towns. Interestingly, with the success of Walton's "brands for less" concept in these areas, he was attacked for "closing down Main Street" and putting the mom-and-pop stores there out of business. Confronted with this attack, Walton, always the insurgent, went on the offensive: "You bet I closed that mom-and-pop store on Main Street, those fine folks who've been charging you a 40 percent markup for the past 25 years!"

Over the last 30 years, we do not know of a single major political campaign that has been won by a candidate who stayed predominately on the defense. Campaigns are won by fighting forward. By playing offense. By being a change leader and by changing the dynamics on which you are strategically focused and on which your success will ultimately depend.

That's the core lesson of these three change leaders—Graham, Burke, and Walton—that you must apply to your own business and world. In other words, *stop acting like a leader.* When someone wearing a pin-striped suit and smoking a big cigar across a mahogany boardroom table says, "Leaders don't do that," you're probably looking at a soon-to-be-former leader.

This, for example, is what former Southwest Airlines CEO Herb Kelleher means when he says: "Don't play *not* to lose—play to *win!*"

CREATE A BIAS FOR ACTION

You want to create an action culture—a culture of people who take the initiative and are willing to take responsibility for their decisions. As stated earlier, the best way to do that is to establish this kind of behavior from the top down. Show that you can play with the "nothing to lose" attitude of the insurgent. Bill Gates, for example, created an atmosphere at Microsoft in which progress is worth risk—even risking everything in order to move forward.

You've got to create an atmosphere that rewards action at every level. Celebrate action—*even when it doesn't result in success.* Celebrate action in the tiniest details as well as the broadest initiatives. As long as the action is not rash or dangerous, make sure it is recognized. Recognize failure, but also recognize a best-efforts attempt to make something happen. Make inaction and indecision uncool in your company. Make it clear that your organization must be making constant progress, constantly moving forward—even if it's only 3 yards at a time.

Meetings are the bane of any organization. Create an action bias for every get-together. No more meetings for the sake of meetings or to use simply as project updates. Demand "action steps" at the end of every meeting and establish a "by when" date to define the "Election Day"—when success absolutely must be achieved on the issues defined. And, by the way, one happy result of this action meeting ethic will be fewer meetings.

Though American business is rife with athletic imagery, these clichés have become clichés because of the easy application of the sports metaphor to business situations. Consider insurgent athletic examples:

- *Consider the sheer stupidity of the "prevent defense."* One team goes ahead by two touchdowns. It's late in the game. The team must win in order to go to the playoffs. So it does what so many teams do: It moves into a prevent defense. Forget the aggressive blitzing. Forget trying to tackle the ball to cause a fumble. Let's just put in a few extra defensive backs and simply hold on to our lead for dear life.

    And how many times have we watched the other team begin to move the ball and score? It's as if the teams were working off a script we've read before. Momentum changes. The team with the lead is being attacked, and it looks confused, off-balance, outmanned, and outplayed. It's forgotten the cardinal rule of insurgency: Protect a lead and you lose it. It's that simple. Don't sit on a lead. Fight forward. Don't play *not* to lose—play to *win*! Play offense.

    Several years ago, sitting in the locker room of one of Pennsylvania's winningest football coaches, Central Bucks West's Mike Pettine, we listened to his half-time locker room speech. It was hard to know that his team had a four-touchdown lead:

    > You're losing. I'm not happy with the way we're playing. We need sharper offense. I'm telling you, we're going to lose this game if you don't get going . . . the other team will get the ball at kickoff . . . and they're going to try and drive it right down your throats and score and . . . if they do, God help you.

    Winners are invariably paranoid. It comes down to the insatiable instinct to always play as if you are behind. And remember: You may be behind—sooner than you'd like. Winners don't really play defense—they play take-away, aggressively going after the ball and trying to force the turnover.

The argument of play offense is embodied in that constant refocus on the attack, on getting more aggressive. In athletic training, there is a concept called "perceived effort." On a scale of 1 to 10, sprinting full out, 100 percent, until you can't go any harder constitutes a 10. An easy warm-up is a 1. And so, the training question is invariably: Where are you in perceived effort? Seldom should you move above 7. That should happen only when you are warm and ready and weeks before a big contest.

In insurgent terms, you always operate above a 7. And you constantly ask your team: Where can we be more aggressive? How can we attack harder? How can we control the dialogue? How can we move more aggressively to the offense?

TAKE WHAT THEY GIVE YOU

As an insurgent, you must make something happen. You must disrupt the marketplace. But you obviously can't do that by force. It makes no sense to define challenges that cannot be overcome. It's no good running your people up a hill they can't take.

Remember the words of the tough-as-nails football coach, Boyd Williams: "Take what they give you!"

His point is to look for the other side's weakness and play to it. In reshuffling their defense to take away that opening, they'll open up another.

The Confederate General Nathan Bedford Forrest—for whom the character Forrest Gump was named—was famous for his motto "be there firstest with the mostest." General Forrest was considered wildly brash—but all of it was strategically calculated. During the Civil War, all intelligence was human. Generally, the cavalry operated as "the eyes of the army." Its job was to skirmish along the enemy line looking for the weak point. So Forrest was not unique in using this tactic. But what set him apart was his boldness in exploiting the weaknesses his cavalry identified. At this point in military history, with no overview intelligence of the enemy, generals never committed more than about a quarter of their forces to any attack, leaving the rest in reserve in case of counterattack or in case of unexpected resistance. General Forrest, by contrast, committed his full force to attacking the enemy line's weak point. The "mostest" in his strategy was as important as the "firstest." And it won many victories.

Before, we cited the "take-what-they-give-you" opportunism of marketers like Red Bull and Arizona Iced Tea (and our friends Joel McCleary's and Brian Lovejoy's drinks that work) against the soft drink industry's giants. The same is true of Sam Walton's rural distribution strategy. And the same is true of Southwest Airlines' avoidance of the major airlines' hubs. When they were smaller companies starting out, each of these companies probably called this strategy "take whatever you can get." Necessity is the mother of invention. Desperation is the daddy. But the insurgent brands in the market's bottom tier create most of the innovative thinking in every category. These days, these insurgents can ride that innovation right to the top.

The big, incumbent brands at the top of the market have the resources to fight the big set-piece infantry battles for the masses. But attrition in these wars is very costly. And these top-tier incumbents find that they're gaining less ground with every charge "over the top." Yes, it's getting to be a lot like trench warfare—except, in today's marketplaces, you have the one or two top-tier brands facing off against each other, trading one or two points of share—and meanwhile, the smaller guerrilla brands are maneuvering around them and decimating their flanks. Increasingly, the big incumbents are trying to match the strategies and tactics of the little insurgents. They're trying to achieve the efficiency and effectiveness of marketing and distribution that the insurgents have. And these big incumbents are quickly developing the motivation to seek opportunity the way the little insurgents do. Their motivation: stark marketplace terror.

DON'T MEET ARMIES WITH ARMIES

The insurgent business doesn't seek confrontation in the marketplace, although it may constantly be on the attack. Rather, the insurgent subscribes to Winston Churchill's advice: "Never go into the water to fight the shark."

Not only does the insurgent avoid confrontation with market leaders, it even refuses to play on these leaders' playing fields. For example, the British Regulars fighting the American Revolutionaries thought the Minutemen were cowardly for firing their muskets from behind a tree. The Americans thought the British were bloody idiots (literally) for lining up in the open like targets at a turkey shoot.

If guerrilla armies are successful, it's because they learn to turn their regular army opponents' strengths into weaknesses. The regular armies have huge advantages in manpower, but equally huge disadvantages in mobility. The regular armies have force, but the guerrilla armies have stealth. The big guys often own the turf—but the revolutionaries often own the hearts and minds of the people on that turf.

Insurgent marketers use these strategic imbalances as a kind of corporate jiujitsu. Little Linux, for example, thrives only because of the size and power of big Microsoft. The craft brews establish their credibility in contrast to Budweiser's mass production. Small, local suppliers out-service their bigger competitors and create differentiation with the flexibility of customized relationship management—compared to the large company's bureaucratic, one-size-fits-all style.

These small, local suppliers frame the marketplace decisions for their customers in terms of these comparisons and contrasts—on the terms that are most favorable to the insurgent. So they turn market strength into a market weakness for the market leaders. And how do you fight that?

In Afghanistan and Iraq, U.S. Spec Ops forces combined the stealth and mobility of insurgents with the ability to call in devastating superpower ordnance. When a market leader acts like an insurgent, it can be an unstoppable force. In fact, it was this combination of revolutionary tactics and superpower resources that made Microsoft virtually unstoppable as it grew from the 1970s through most of the 1990s. And this kind of success, the Clinton Justice Department decided, was unfair.

The problem is that most market-leading incumbents are simply not training or equipping their troops to fight a new kind of warfare. It's akin to Douglas MacArthur's complaint after being named commandant of the U.S. Military Academy in 1932: "We're still planning to win the war of 1812."

Most big companies in global markets are constantly preparing to fight the last war—the war of mass marketing. To beat them, never fight on their terms or on their turf. Instead, represent everything they are not; meet their market tactics not with the same, but with the opposite.

This may be considered the "new" marketing, but it has been winning revolutions for three thousand years.

TAKE CONTROL OF THE DIALOGUE AND NEVER LET GO

As we've said before in this book and will say again and again (and again and again), the candidate who controls the dialogue will win the election. Control the market dialogue and you win the market.

In today's reset environment, this control is gained by change. Moreover, the good news for the insurgent is that *the incumbent doesn't want to change and will resist changing at almost all costs.* And this gives you a hell of an advantage. It's like knowing that the champ won't throw the left, so you keep circling to the right and hooking your right. You'll tear him up.

If the incumbent hates change, then you, as the insurgent, must love it. Of course, beware the incumbent who comes to love change, like, for example, Frito-Lay. Getting control away from this kind of incumbent market leader is going to be very, very difficult.

Another assumption that you can make as the insurgent marketer is that *the incumbent has fallen behind the change in consumer attitudes.* Today, in virtually every marketplace, consumers' desires for refreshment and change are greater than, and move ahead of, the incumbent's willingness to provide it. This is all part of the incumbent's general aversion to change.

For decades, the biggest companies, the market leaders, didn't necessarily have to innovate because of their marketplace domination. When change was forced upon them by the innovations of a market insurgent, these market leaders simply followed the change, eventually overtaking and trampling the smaller competitor. But today, the problem for these market leaders is that market change is moving much faster. And so is viral communication about change.

Today, the early adopter segment in every marketplace is instantly informed about new choices and is very quick to move to them—and indeed the magnetic pull of big brands on these early adopters is weaker than ever. The current "cycle of newness" is compressed; the next round of changes in the market value proposition and the next and the next come faster and faster as more and more new ideas are introduced. Contrast this to only a decade or so ago, when a newly introduced product advantage might enjoy a year without matching competition. Today, however, that time has shortened—first to 6 months, then to 13 weeks, then to a month, and now, in many cases, to just a few days or hours. Often, the enormous consumer demand at high early adopter margins is devoured by the small insurgents before the lumbering giants can move to it. And the successful insurgent takes this market foothold and continues to grow—and grow.

Fundamentally, then, the way to control the dialogue is to drive change ahead of what consumers are thinking. And the nature of this change should be dictated by a better understanding of the consumer's wants and needs than the incumbents are able or willing to develop. In fact, a deft insurgent should be able to find a way to fit into the gap between what consumers really want and need and what the incumbent is willing or able to deliver.

Here are three fundamentally important ways in which insurgents drive this marketplace change and control the dialogue:

- *Define yourself.* Your company's system—your workers, board of directors, sales force, investors, alliance partners, constituents, early adopters, and so on—must understand the company culture as an extension of its leader's personality, character, vision, and values. In all internal communications, your own beliefs and principles must be clearly defined—to be fully energized, your entire company system must know not only *what* you believe but *why* you believe it. They don't need to know what you will decide in every situation. But they must understand *how* you will decide it, what it is within you that drives every decision.

- *Define your business.* In the midst of today's information clutter, you must define your brand and your business with extraordinary efficiency and effectiveness. This definition must be built around a very crisp understanding of what your business does in terms of delivering benefits to its customers. Every communication, every interaction, every advertisement must flow from this meaning and reflect it, being derived from a clear and disciplined business and brand definition that comes from you directly. In Jim Collins's superb book *Good to Great: Why Some Companies Make the Leap and Others Don't,* he argues exhaustively that the companies that sustain greatness do three things better than their competitors. Specifically, they define:

    What they can do best in the world—understanding at the same time what they cannot do best in the world

    What drives their economic engine—attaining penetrating insight into what generates their own cash flow and profitability

    What they are deeply passionate about—focusing on activities that ignite their organizational passion

In other words, great companies define their business and brand with an aggressive discipline and clarity—they win by the power of their own definition of what they do and how they will ultimately succeed.

- *Define the future.* As discussed in Chapter 2, it's the prerogative of any market leader to define the future of its industry. Yet, this opportunity is seldom seized.

In fact, insurgent leaders don't only affect the future— they help define it. Look at some companies that have done just this. American Airlines's frequent flyer program and Merrill Lynch's CMA defined the future of their marketplaces. Again, look at Microsoft: Over the years, Chairman Bill Gates's leadership challenge hasn't only involved defining the future for his employees; more importantly, it has entailed defining the future for the industry itself, and for the larger marketplace in which the company competes. Every day, Gates continues to literally define the future of this larger marketplace—for example, smiling on the cover of the November 2003 *Newsweek* underneath the headline: "BILL'S NEXT BIG THING: Gates on the Future of Computers."

This is the same as in politics. There is an old saying in campaigns: Frame the decision, and you win the election. In other words, define the future context and you win the opportunity to control it. For example:

> *In 1992, the successful Clinton communications context was the national economy.* Every issue and every communication from his campaign was framed in the context of its effect on the economy. The internal theme: "It's the Economy, Stupid!"

> *In 1996, Clinton took advantage of voters' concerns over congressional Republican cutbacks and established a new context: "If you believe we should not cut Medicaid, Medicare, the environment, and education, then you can't be a Republican."* This formed the con-

textual theme for the entire campaign and every issue within it—and, importantly, was believed by a wide majority of Americans.

In 1997, South Korea's Kim Dae Jung was the 72-year-old opposition candidate from the widely unpopular Cholla region who had previously lost three national elections and was considered too radical to be elected. But his campaign took advantage of Kim's age and his nation's economic crisis by strategically defining Koreans' context of choice: "In these extraordinary times, this election is about choosing the most prepared man to govern the nation."

In 1999, candidate and client Chen Shui Bian won by defining what the election was all about: "Who's strong enough to bring real democracy to Taiwan?" In 1999, candidate and client Vicente Fox won by asking Mexican voters: "Who can bring real change to our nation?" And, in 2002, candidate and client Roh Moo Hyun won by framing the electoral question on his own terms: "Who can best clean up corrupt, old-style politics and prepare Korea for a great future?"

In the end, then, you must define on your own terms the context in which you will compete. Define yourself—and, whatever you do, don't let the competition do it for you. Define your business. Define the future. And finally, define success. Ultimately, that's the best way to win in today's hypercompetitive marketplace.

SUSTAIN THE ATTACK

The most devastating punch in boxing is not the "haymaker" but the jab. Eventually, it is the constant irritation, frustration, and disorientation created by the jab that opens up an opportunity for a much easier knockout. Too often, however, the jab is not sustained. It's used too infrequently to truly disrupt an opponent's fight plan. Again, too often, this is the case with insurgents' attacks on marketplace incumbents: Even when these insurgents' attacks are successful, they're too seldom sustained. There's too little follow-through.

The insurgent therefore needs to be mobile, agile, and hostile and must be constantly improvising—developing and driving a sustained plan of attack:

- This means marshalling your resources so that you can attack and attack and attack again over a 12-month calendar.
- This means developing a 12-month pipeline of product changes/refreshments or new product introductions.
- And, again, this means creating a sense of momentum from inside-out: from your own team, your "friends and family," and your first line of loyal customers. They must all feel forward and sustained movement.

CELEBRATE EVERY WIN

The insurgent always fights the battle on the field and in the minds of the citizenry. This insurgent must win both substantive and emotional victories. In fact, throughout business, political, and military history, it's this sense of emotional victory, a victory for a cause greater than one's self, which motivates the sacrifices necessary for the revolutionary to succeed.

- *In business, every win is another proof point that communicates from the inside out*—and through the insurgent company to its system partners to its stakeholders and to and through its customers. "Maybe we *can* do it!"
- *In business, every win is an upset victory.* Every win builds confidence and strength. Each successive win helps solidify a culture of success. True insurgents commemorate every success:

  In the 1970s, Mary Wells, of the storied Wells, Rich, Greene agency, revolutionized the advertising industry. Wells used to employ one secretary full time just to find meaningful gifts for her talented and hardworking people—and for those among the agency's system partners and stakeholders, including clients, who contributed and deserved to share in its success.

A successful insurgent company in another industry keeps a trophy case of empty champagne bottles, each with the specific achievement it celebrated and a commemorative date written in gold ink on the dark green bottle. These tokens take on religious significance among the insurgents—the symbols of their revolution and success.

NEVER ACT LIKE THE INCUMBENT

History and fiction are filled with stories of the humble, hardworking challenger who becomes the champ and "forgets where he came from." In fiction at least, the wayward insurgent comes to his or her senses just before the final credits roll. History, however, is not so kind to insurgents who take on the character of the incumbents they replace. Here's how to avoid that terrible fate for yourself and your company:

- *Never, ever declare victory.* Celebrate the small victories, but never declare the war won—this was George W. Bush's single greatest mistake about the war Iraq. Keep the spirit of battle and the smell of napalm in the air.
- *Don't stop setting doable goals.* After several doable goals have been achieved, managers often slack off: "Okay, we got it now." But nobody tires of achievement. Keep setting up goals. Keep knocking them down.
- *Don't let anybody get between you and your customers.* Stay on them like holy on the Pope. Understand these customers' needs so well that you anticipate them. How? Make sure you're in a constant, fluid dialogue with them.
- *Don't stop hating "bigness."* Most companies hate big, bureaucratic companies until they get to be one. But keep that

instinct alive in yourself and your people. Don't just hate big-ness—fight it at every opportunity. Don't take on any of the trappings or fall into any of the bureaucratic traps of big com-panies. Keep the organization as flat as you can; few, for example, are flatter than News Corporation—and few retain their best people and fighting spirit better than this consis-tently successful insurgent company.

JUST DO IT

Play offense. Insurgent tactics will get you control of the market dialogue, and never let go.

- Ride ahead of today's waves of change.
- Define yourself—before your opponent can do so.
- Get scared. And stay scared.
- Don't play *not* to lose—play to *win*.
- When in doubt, play offense.

Steps

- Define your destination.
- Define your source of business (your "SOB"); where's your growth coming from?
- Define your market targets. And remember to define them by atti-tude.
- Define your five key brand dimensions.
- Define your strategy.
- Ratchet up your "perceived effort" of execution.
- Leverage and win on speed, sustenance, emotion, localness, clarity, and relative strength.

Exercises

- Map out the forces of change in your marketplace over the next decade. List them in order of magnitude.

- Define your brand destination. Refer to your conviction statement from Chapter 2 and write down in detail what success will look like 10 years from today. Write down what you want to be when you grow up.
- Define your SOB. Whose hide is it coming out of?
- Define your market targets and both how and whether they're likely to vote.
- Define your brand across the five key dimensions:

    Presence

    Relevance

    Differentiation

    Credibility

    Imagery

- Define yourself. What do you stand for? What do you believe, deep down, most passionately? What drives you every day? Write one to two pages on this definition.
- Define your enemy. Who are you against? What are you not? Who is the incumbent in your market against which you can position yourself for success?
- Define your business. With your core team's help, answer three key questions: At what can you be the best in the world? What fuels your economic engine—specifically, your future net cash flow? And, finally, about what do you believe passionately?
- Define the future. What will your industry look like 10 years from now? And how are you helping to define its future? Go back to your "do the doable" competitive map and answers and apply them here.
- Internally, invest in a 30-day "listening tour" within your organization. Every day, make at least three "how-are-you-doing?" calls to friends, family, board members, key employees, and high-volume customers.
- Drive the "by when" discipline into your organizational culture—never let a meeting end before participants agree on who will do what *by when*.
- Create a "perceived effort" continuum from easy to totally aggressive and identify ways to move harder to the offense in key insurgent areas: speed, sustenance, emotion, localness, clarity, and relative strength.

5

Communicate Inside-Out

"Dance with the girl that brung ya."

—COACH BEAR BRYANT

➢ *Sell your own employees before you try to sell anyone else.*

➢ *Monitor closely what your employees really believe; their reality is the foundation for your strategy.*

➢ *Overcommunicate key themes and messages.*

➢ *Learn "inside-out leadership" from three insurgents: Kelleher, Welch, and Gates.*

➢ *Create customer satisfaction "inside-out" like Southwest Airlines does.*

Political campaigns run on the energy and dedication of volunteers and underpaid, overstressed staff. They know that long before they can move voters, they must move the people who will move the voters. This means communicating and motivating "inside-out."

But most companies forget this key principle. While focusing on market targets, they neglect key constituents who will ultimately be responsible for delivering on their brands' promises to those market targets. So, fundamental to insurgent behavior is the need to ensure that every member of your organization—from the very bottom up—understands and believes in your core strategy. In Chapter 7, we'll show you the importance of controlling the meaning of even the tiniest details—because it's the details that define brands and brand experiences for consumers, distributors, and all other stakeholders. Execution is the critical last few yards of the football field for your strategy. And execution is up to the people in your company and your extended system. Selling your strategy inside-out is the only way you can ensure execution . . . getting the ball into the end zone.

To drive your strategy to successful execution, you must begin at the very beginning by communicating the company's mission and core inside-out. This communication must begin with the innermost circle of a leader's office and move person-to-person to his or her executive committee, senior officers, managers, partners, employees, salespeople, board of directors, strategic allies, shareholders, analysts, journalists, opinion leaders, community leaders, former employees, constituents, customers, and prospects. Again and again, we've found that employees can, and must, become an organization's strongest communications and marketing medium.

Look, for example, at IBM's problems throughout the 1980s— the computer giant literally fell apart from the inside out. It had a confused mission, an unfocused strategy, lackluster employee attitudes, and an outdated culture—played out in undifferentiated products and strategies in the marketplace. It took Lou Gerstner in the early 1990s to refocus and reenergize its employees from the inside out and reclaim IBM's great success and legacy. To understand the power of Gerstner's inside-out success, consider the view of IBM in the 1980s as a powerless, slothful giant; its employees one rung up from those of the Postal Service. Under Gerstner's command, a few hundred employees were fired (under his predecessor, remember, thousands had been laid off), and a few score of new "Gerstnerites" were hired. But it was the thousands of long-term IBM employees who turned the company around, by turning around their perceptions of themselves, the company, and their conviction to succeed. They went from worst to first by creating an insurgent strategy from the inside out.

Look, too, at The Coca-Cola Company. For nearly 7 years, we watched the worst of incumbent instincts allow the world's largest beverage company to ignore the Pepsi Challenge in the 1970s. They said: "Leaders don't recognize the attack of an also-ran—that's just giving them free advertising." And they said: "Consumers don't like comparative advertising." And, of course, they maintained: "The Pepsi Challenge isn't really hurting us anyway." So Pepsi attacked. And attacked. And attacked. And Coke, with the arrogance and over-confidence that can curse an incumbent, pretended it didn't matter.

Indeed, Pepsi's share gains from its challenge didn't come directly from Coca-Cola. The Pepsi Challenge was launched in Coke's heartland, where Pepsi's place in the market was not number two, but number five or six. Pepsi's growth came first at the expense of numbers four, three, and two in that heartland marketplace. But this represented Coke's potential for market growth, too. So Pepsi was literally challenging The Coca-Cola Company's future. And the Pepsi Challenge created enormous consumer trial; even more important, it created enormous belief and energy within the Pepsi bottling system. A typical strategy session in a bottling plant during the Pepsi Challenge consisted of rewarding route salespeople by giving them free sledgehammer whacks at a Coke vending machine.

Then, finally, Coke decided to fight back. The impetus for its response was the proliferation of taste tests and challenges among almost every cola in the marketplace, following Pepsi's insurgent lead. Brands like Royal Crown, Bubble Up, and Cott were taking on Coke in their own taste tests. In response, Coke hired Bill Cosby as a spokesman. It used his talent and credibility brilliantly, asking a simple question and providing the inescapable conclusion: "Why do you think everybody's doing taste tests against Coca-Cola? Maybe that's why they call Coke, 'The Real Thing.'"

The effect of this response worked inside-out. It reenergized beleaguered line and sales employees, giving them a sense of fighting back: There couldn't be a challenger if Coke wasn't the champ. First, and foremost, it mobilized the company's vast internal system: employees, distributors' employees, retail and fountain customers' employees, partners, co-promoters, core customers, and so on.

Cosby, an astute insurgent businessman himself, took the time to develop the internal marketing campaign for the response to the Pepsi Challenge, shooting specific commercials for employees and system partners. The effect moved in ripples through the system and out to Coke's most loyal customers. And the reaction of these consumers to Cosby's advertising was almost unanimous: "It's about time!" They complained that they'd been constantly challenged themselves, "Why are you still drinking Coke?" Cosby gave them the answer.

THREE KEY INSIDE GROUPS

By "inside," of course, we don't just mean employees. We include three important groups in this definition: employees, system partners, and "friends and family."

- *Employees.* These are the core—their commitment, energy, and focus determine your productivity. They are ultimately responsible for your products and brands and for delivering the brand promise.
- *System partners.* These must make a commitment to deliver that brand promise in the marketplace. These system partners may be suppliers, wholesale or retail distributors, marketing partners, sponsored events or individuals, industry organizations, or investors. They must feel that they own your strategy and own its success. At The Coca-Cola Company, the saying goes: "Sell the system; the system will sell the Coke."

- *Friends and family.* These are the extended family of your company and brand, often called stakeholders. These may be the families of employees, community leaders, industry leaders, mentors, "soft and hard support" analysts, investors and journalists, and that first line of loyalist customers. These "insiders," too, must understand your strategy and help communicate your key themes and messages. They want to root for the home team, but they don't start cheering until they see some first downs. You need to give them plenty of reasons to cheer.

These three groups are the most important and often most overlooked constituents of any company or brand. You've heard the expression "that's just preaching to the choir," as if selling your company's vision, product concepts, and strategies to those who already have a vested interest in the company is a waste of time and money. But, in fact, preaching to the converted (or nearly converted, Chapter 3's soft supporters inside your own organization and distribution system) is what turns them into evangelists. That's the basic energy source of evangelical Christianity.

Of course, selling inside-out is a core principle of the Islamist extremists: Instead of spending time, effort, and treasure trying to convert those whom they consider to be infidels, they focus constant attention on their own true believers, pushing their faith into fanaticism. The objective is to create jihadists, those few who, through military means, will provide the infidels with the choice of conversion or death. Consider the many months the radical Islamist leadership focused intensely on developing homicide bombers.

It's becoming clear that they have done too good a job. By making suicide the ultimate proof of faith, the Islamist leaders and the state-funded madrassas have developed an extended pipeline of willing young recruits. It helps to have an extensive population of young people in authoritarian, oligarchic, and theocratic societies who have few hopes—the ideal candidates for suicidal commitment to an afterlife of bread, wine, and endless babes. But one result is to diminish the impact of the homicide bombing by overuse of the tactic. It has become an anonymous act, despite the best efforts of the Islamists to glorify the atrocity. Further, it's not brilliant military strategy. General George Patton said: "The idea is not to die for your country. The idea is to get the other dumb son of a bitch to die for his country." You have to wonder if even bin Laden and Zawahiri sometimes sit in their dank mountain hiding holes and question the results of their 9/11 strategy for their ultimate cause.

In civilized society, particularly in the West but increasingly in Asia, selling inside-out is harder than ever. Institutional loyalty used to be a given. Today, it's a rarity. To be fair and balanced, you'd have to admit that it was corporations' massive disloyalty to employees in the 1980s and 1990s that created the equal force of employee disloyalty to companies. Even in Japan, the "salary man" is an endangered species. In today's "reset" environment, in which every relationship—institutional, company, brand, or personal—is being reconsidered, it's harder than ever to develop commitment among insiders. So selling inside-out is more important than ever. Most managers believe that their job is to develop company plans, and everybody else's job is to carry them out. In this reset environment, you can't expect blind faith and unquestioning commitment. Sergio Zyman calls it the "Why Generation." And management's job is to provide the answers for, "What do we do . . . really? Why is it important? What's our long-term vision and strategy? Why should I believe that our strategy will work? And what's my part in the big picture at this company?"

UNDERSTAND THE WORLD ON ITS TERMS

Ideally, using the principles of inside-out communications, you'll answer those questions *before* they're asked.

Over two decades of work, we've learned that energizing an organization's internal culture demands communicating and reinforcing employees' core values—their sense of what the company believes and the values for which the brand stands. This means defining your organization's *conviction* and the larger *context* of why these employees come to work each day, adrenalized about their own success as a part of the organization's success.

"Success cultures" within which we have worked create an emotional context and an environment of excitement and open communication. They stand for something far larger than the actual products they make and the services they provide. Nike stands for unbending excellence on every playing field; Coke stands for the refreshment of mind, body, and spirit in everything it does. Chip Coe's great little company, Smartwool of Colorado, makes socks and underclothes for skiers and hikers. His people firmly believe their fanatical dedication to quality has a direct relationship to the skier's performance.

In other words, your job as a manager is to adopt this book's core argument and wage the equivalent of an insurgent and ongoing campaign inside your own organization to assure your ultimate success.

That's management of the insurgent business. Our next chapter (Chapter 6, "Forget Reality: Perceptions Rule") will deal with the need to learn to base your strategy on the perceptions of the constituents who will have to accept and deliver the strategy. We are strong believers in probing market research to define the perceptions and attitudes of all key market targets. Like everything else in insurgent strategy, research begins inside and works its way out. The most important perceptions and attitudes are those within the organization: those of employees, market partners, and the extended friends and family.

Here's the rule you must understand and obey—a rule as certain as gravity: Perceptions create attitudes, and attitudes create behavior. So the behavior you need is a result of the right attitudes shaped by the right perceptions.

- *Understanding insiders' perceptions and attitudes will be the foundation for the development of your inside-out strategy.* So turn the microscope around. Define these insiders' most basic perceptions and attitudes: What do we do; what makes our company/products/services/brands unique; what are you most proud of/most ashamed of in your work; what's your part in the process? Effective strategy is impossible without this information and analysis. In fact, one of our clients has for many years used research among employees and recruits as an "early warning system" on the corporate brand's strengths and weaknesses—this is where problems and opportunities first show up on the radar screen.

- *Develop attitudinal segmentation among employee and market partner groups.* This includes hard opposition, soft opposition, undecided, soft support, and hard support. This will tell you where to focus your communications for the greatest effect. It will define who will carry your messages most productively. And it will show you where to look for trouble before it happens.

DEVELOP A 3 × 5–CARD DISCIPLINE

The principles you've learned in the first four chapters (adopt the political campaign model, do the doable, move the movable, and play offense) should be applied inside-out. They were designed for any group, institution, battlefield, or marketplace. What appeals to us about applying the campaign model to business is the close fit of campaign orthodoxy to the total needs of a business. Many businesses use one set of principles for management (often, every top manager has her or his own adopted set of strategic principles), another for HR, another for marketing, another for manufacture, another for organization.

That's why the typical business management style and strategic approach looks like a business bookshelf at Barnes & Noble: There are quite different approaches standing side by side. And the result is uneven, like a tract house built on an unstable foundation with cracks running up the walls from the basement.

Insurgent political strategy applies to the total business, across every aspect of operations and communications. Everybody will understand the concepts.

From your core strategy, you will have developed a messaging discipline, the key themes and messages that define your company and brand as relevant and different for all constituents.

- *Sell the strategy inside-out.* If your own people can't simply, quickly, and compellingly relate the company strategy and brand meaning, then there is zero chance of getting the strategy and brand into the marketplace in one piece. *This is not about telling employees what to do; it's about selling them on what can be done.* Management must take the time to transfer ownership of the company strategy and brand positioning to key groups within the company and the system. Here, too, if management can't sell it to insiders, don't expect better results on the outside.

- *Create a 3 × 5–card communications discipline.* That means distilling the key themes and messages of your core strategy into the simplicity and power defined by one side of a 3 × 5 card. When you transfer ownership of the company or brand strategy, provide 3 × 5 cards for all employees. This is the same card and the same message that is in the CEO's pocket. Salespeople should paste it up by the phone or laptop. The discipline is that you must communicate these four or five points in every conversation and presentation—in everything you say and do. Of course, you can say more. You must provide depth and substance on certain aspects of the message for specific audiences (like customers), but you won't deviate from the plan. Your strategy in the marketplace will be only as successful as you are in developing this discipline inside-out.

LEADING INSIDE-OUT

Let's look at three of the best insurgent, inside-out leaders of the last quarter century.

Herb Kelleher: Creating "Living Advertisements"

If ever there were a master of viral marketing, it was Southwest Airlines' founding CEO, Herb Kelleher. From that fateful day in 1966 when Kelleher and other Southwest Airlines' founders drew a triangle with Dallas, San Antonio, and Houston on the back of a Jack Daniel's–stained cocktail napkin, Kelleher virtually rewrote the airline industry's rulebook.

To this day, Southwest remains the top airline in the United States according to annual consumer satisfaction research and profitability, as well. In fact, Southwest is a paragon of customer satisfaction among all industries, even though it operates in the industry that leads the universe in customer dissatisfaction. In the process, Southwest has cleared the way for other insurgents, like Jet Blue, AirTran, and Midwest Express.

We've analyzed the way Southwest creates customer satisfaction and loyalty. It's become the insurgent model, and we describe it with a formula that we call DOCS:

$$D + O + C = S$$

> D = define expectations in advance
> O = overdeliver on a key benefit
> C = constantly remind customers of what you've done for them
> S = satisfaction, success, $s

- *Define expectations in advance.* In the early 1990s, we studied customer satisfaction for Microsoft. The low customer satisfaction scores for its applications software puzzled the company. After all, for all the jokes about buggy Microsoft products at introduction, the company is fanatically dedicated to constant product improvement. (Our observation is that two principles keep this focus on product and customer: "the product is never finished" and "the sale is never final.") In market research, customers told Microsoft that they simply didn't know how to judge the software: "You keep telling us how fast and powerful it is. But what does that mean to me?"

We realized that customer satisfaction can't be delivered unless the product's benefits are defined in advance. You've got to shape customer expectations if you're going to deliver customer satisfaction. You've got to tell customers the benefits you'll deliver to them (and not just the attributes you deliver to your product).

Southwest defines these expectations clearly: "cheap, frequent flights between business destinations; no frills and no B.S."

It's notable what Southwest *doesn't* promise: first-class seats or upgrades, gourmet meals or wine, fawning service. Also notable is the parenthetic promise of Southwest's history: A bargain airline must establish credibility on the issue of safety, and Southwest has an exemplary record.

- *Overdeliver on a key benefit.* You've undoubtedly noticed that Southwest's defined expectations are pretty modest. That's the core of its "no frills and no B.S." philosophy and value proposition. Contrast that to the way the biggies (United, Delta, American, Continental, or US Airways) define expectations. You've seen their commercials. There's always a guy (first expectation: If you fly on business, you're a guy) sitting in first or business class, tie loosened, relaxing in comfort, the seat next to him empty and a beautiful flight attendant handing him a goblet of fine wine. When have you actually experienced what that commercial defines? The two of us are about 0-for-6 million miles on that experience. How about you? And how can the airline possibly deliver on that expectation?

Southwest doesn't promise much; and certainly doesn't make the overpromises of the big airlines. Indeed, it establishes their meaning in absolute contrast to the big guys. Its "cheap, frequent flights" aren't necessarily even the cheapest: On a given day, one of the big airlines may beat Southwest with a special deal (which accounts for the slob sitting next to you who paid three or four hundred dollars less than you for the same class of service you get). Southwest uses an everyday low price, with much less frequent (but commensurately much more meaningful) sales events. In this way, Southwest delivers on expectations. But that's not enough. To win customer satisfaction in a sophisticated and cynical marketplace, you have to overdeliver. Southwest overdelivers on service attitude. It's legendary at the airline (one pictures, but may never have actually seen, the pilot carrying bags to the aircraft). Of course, it helps that the gate agents don't have to argue with customers over seat assignments or upgrades: There aren't any. Southwest hires service personnel based on attitude, not just aptitude. And it works. Southwest overdelivers on service. It's a high-importance benefit. And, for frequent business travelers, the no B.S. approach is just as relevant.

Think about the viral marketing power of all this. Several years ago, one of those overpromising airlines conducted a study and found that for every customer who said that he or she felt underdelivered to and complained, 25 others felt the same way but remained silent. Each of these 26 customers told an average of 12 of their friends. Underdeliver and over 300 people hear about it.

- *Constantly remind customers of what you've done for them.* Southwest and other business insurgents abandon subtlety in reminding customers of what they've done for them. This requires the same kind of simplicity and compelling power as the 3 × 5–card messaging: Remind them of the few things you do that provide relevant benefits that are clearly different from your competitors. The clichéd captain's announcement when the big airlines land in one of their voraciously protected hubs drives any business flyer nuts: "We realize you have a choice when you travel. . . ." What choice? Greyhound?

A major lesson to draw from Kelleher's brilliant inside-out leadership is DOC. For example, we often work with our clients to develop a series of "proof points" that are spaced strategically within a pipeline to create maximum perceptual effect in the eyes of the audience. Define the expectation. Overdeliver on the expectation. Claim the overdelivery.

And, importantly, don't forget to stop and claim, or, better, celebrate, this success. We love, for example, the story of the Four Seasons several years ago. The leading high-end hotel chain realized that across the eight service categories that customers said were most important, the Four Seasons was far and away leading its competition in five areas—but, surprisingly, was well behind in the other three. What did the company do? For months, it decided to ask every customer at checkout to rate how the hotel had performed—but only in the five areas in which the company knew it was leading. A brilliant way to remind every customer on every checkout about every single overdelivery.

Of course, over the years at Southwest, Herb Kelleher did more than invent and discipline the customer satisfaction process from the inside out. Indeed, more than any other airline head, Kelleher energized his 20,000-plus employees and made each one of them an individual point of difference. As he describes it, every employee must become "a living advertisement." And, as an insurgent leader, Kelleher's job was to deploy every tactical advantage to communicate and motivate from the inside out. For example, Kelleher:

- *Created a "small company" and compelling atmosphere for employees,* best summed up in the words of one employee, who said, "Southwest Airlines is enough fun that it almost makes you feel guilty to call it work."

- *Demanded that meetings be action-oriented*, with clear agendas, moments of decision, and forward progress. The words "let's study this" were banned from the company's culture.

- *Ensured that all communications were short, clear, and to the point,* including the company's fun and compelling corporate newsletter, *LUV LINES.*

- *Created a "culture committee"* to, in effect, act as ongoing ambassadors, missionaries, and storytellers within the company's culture.

- *Celebrated spectacularly every overdelivery of every goal,* with Kelleher as not only the top leader, but also the most enthusiastic cheerleader.

- *Distributed a new and reenergized mission statement inside a Crackerjack box* as a novel and metaphorical "prize" for every single employee, thus generating a humorous, positive, and lasting word of mouth.

- *Transferred ownership of this revised mission statement to as many employees as possible* through constant dialogue, communicating real-life case studies, and encouraging entrepreneurial behaviors.

In short, Kelleher gave employees permission to play to win and to act like owners of the company. He embodied Wal-Mart's Sam Walton's motto: "The more they know, the more they care." And he understood the power of inside-out communications and creating living advertisements to define your organization's future success.

Jack Welch: Creating an Honest Dialogue

Over 20 years as CEO, Jack Welch built General Electric into a company with a market capitalization of $450 billion and into one of the world's most admired brands. Developing and using his famous "Six

Sigma" quality system, focusing globally, and vowing to "fix, sell, or close each business," in many ways Welch helped define today's modern corporation.

From Welch's original "vision" speech on December 8, 1981, the corporate head understood the power of inside-out leadership in at least three ways:

- First, he prioritized inside-out *leadership* and communications, summed-up in a philosophy of "people first; strategy second." For example, Welch initiated cutting-edge employee research as a "B.S. detector," asking simply: "Is the company you read about in the annual report the company you work for?" Moreover, from the very beginning, Welch took the time to send surprisingly personal, handwritten annual review letters to each of his senior officers.

- Second, from the inside-out Welch created a novel and powerful "honest dialogue" to improve organizational efficiency and effectiveness. This involved "work-out" sessions—beginning in the famous Crotonville Pit and ultimately reaching, by 1992, an amazing 200,000 employees. These work-out sessions, patterned after traditional New England town meetings, involved 40 to 100 workers who shared their views and suggestions with management over 2 to 3 days. At first, no boss was present. A facilitator encouraged workers to speak frankly and honestly. The goal was to find ways to eliminate extra bureaucracy and administrative red tape—hence the name "work-out." Soon, the boss came into the meeting, with the proviso that decisions on each proposal would be made on the spot—or, in 25 percent of the cases, on an agreed-upon and not-too-distant date.

  It worked. It drove boundaryless behavior across the departmental stovepipes that can become the curse of every incumbent company we advise. A work-out session developed ideas. It converted General Electric's culture into a more aggressive, entrepreneurial, energized, and unified team of people.

- Third, Welch understood a lesson from the political campaign world in terms of the power of communicating *repetitively* a simple, focused set of themes and messages: In fact, the moment you are absolutely sick of hearing yourself say something, one more person will be hearing it for the first time. As Welch writes in his best-selling book *Jack: Straight From the Gut*:

> Whenever I had an idea or message I wanted to drive into the organization, I could never say it enough. I repeated it over and over and over, at every meeting and review, for years, until I could almost gag on the words.

There is power in repetition. In fact, there's an old saying: "You have to say something ten times before someone actually hears it the first time." Welch understood the all-too-frequent truth of this and, by driving an honest dialogue and communicating with the disciplined repetition of a great political candidate, he built the General Electric of today.

Bill Gates: Re-recruiting His Best People

Microsoft Chairman Bill Gates is a master of an important aspect of inside-out communications that he calls "re-recruiting." The point is to reengage your most talented people again and again. It's about re-wooing a long-term mate. It's about keeping the spark in the romance. For Microsoft, that spark is achieved by personal achievement and gain, but also by being a part of a bigger vision. Gates created an aggressive and highly competitive culture (just ask former Attorney General Janet Reno). In the early days, he was committed to creating competition within the company that would translate into more aggressive action externally. He'd pit the business units against one another to compete for funding.

In many ways, that created a ruthlessness that was parallel to aggressiveness. And Bill realized that it made the company a tough and demanding place to work. As we've said again and again, no company we've ever worked with appreciates its human capital more than Microsoft. It always seeks the best, in the tradition of the famous Dallas Cowboys' Tex Schramm, looking in every round of the NFL draft not for a specific position player, but for the best available athlete. Microsoft goes for intellectual power in its recruits. Recruiting is not enough. You must constantly re-recruit the best of them, reestablishing the covenant they have with the company and focusing on making very clear the significant part they play in meeting the overall challenges Microsoft faces. As McDonald's Ray Kroc would say, Gates clearly believes that "none of us is as important as all of us." And, at the individual level, Microsoft carefully manages the career paths of those "re-recruits," the irreplaceable 1500 or 2000 top employees (not necessarily the top managers, by the way).

Gates understands, too, the power of customers as the most powerful form of advertising—viral, word-of-mouth testimony. Microsoft, in fact, identifies and targets strategically "influential end users" (IEUs). These market targets are not official information technology managers; rather, they're the people down the hall you go to with questions when you have a problem with your laptop or PDA. They self-identify in Microsoft research by answering the question: "Do you influence more purchases than you make yourself?" These IEUs are powerful viral marketers and provide the credible testimonials in any marketplace. In many ways, this is the best marketing Microsoft has ever used. Even today, it ripples outward through employees, to system partners to friends and family, on to IEUs, and through them to the rest of the market.

Microsoft's objectives are selling in depth and breadth—selling each customer every new release or upgrade of a product (depth) and selling each customer more products along the Microsoft line (breadth). Selling IEUs first is the key to achieving these objectives.

HOW DO YOU ACTUALLY DO THIS?

O.K., you're sold. You've bought inside-out communicating. You appreciate the power of viral communications. You know you can't win in the marketplace until you win in your own company and system.

Let's review in "nine easy pieces":

1. *You must sell your own employees before you can sell anyone else.* You must define your internal marketing plan and execute it before you move to the marketplace.

2. *Assume that your employees are sophisticated and cynical.* Build your brand with them the way you will with customers: create relevance, differentiation, and credibility wrapped in powerful imagery.

3. *Never tell them; sell them.* The best way to do that is to transfer ownership of strategy and tactical plans to them. Keep an open dialogue going during strategy formation—listen to and incorporate their ideas. Make your success their success. Transfer ownership right through employees, system partners, friends and family, and the rest of the marketplace.

4. *Monitor employees' perceptions and attitudes closely.* Use the same market research techniques inside as you would outside the company.

   An expert who understands inside-out communications better than anyone else, Rob Smith, the founder of Focal Point, developed an employee program that utilized research to identify three attitudinal categories inside a company that was making the transition from an old to a new, more competitive culture:

   Frozen. These employees were stuck in a past culture and were stubbornly unwilling to change their behavior or focus on the company's new challenges and mission. These workers were hard and soft opposition to the new CEO's plans.

   Unfrozen. These employees had thawed from the beliefs of the past, but had not yet made up their minds or become convinced about the company's new challenges and mission. These workers were undecided.

Refrozen. These employees had been re-formed in the new culture and were immediately supportive of and on board with the new CEO's strategy and focus. These workers were natural insurgents, and it was on their shoulders that the company's success most immediately rested.

Successful employee communications entails targeting and mobilizing "refrozen" employees—hard supporters, as we call them—because it is these workers who are likely to begin to pull the "unfrozen," or undecided, workers along with them. Ultimately, these "refrozen" employees will self-select into something similar to Southwest Airlines' culture committee and drive the new CEO and the company to long-term success.

5. *Overcommunicate key themes and messages.* Tell them. Tell them you told them. Tell them again. Create a 3 × 5–card discipline for the core messages of the company and its brands.

6. *Create employee satisfaction the way you create customer satisfaction,* by defining expectations in advance, overdelivering on a key benefit, and not only constantly reminding them of what you've done for them but also reminding them of what you're doing together, making them a part of the revolution.

7. *Make sure you can define your business insurgency and market revolution* in a "what we believe" speech. As in Chapter 2, the format:

Conviction. The compelling statement of what you believe and the way you see the outside world. This must appeal to the existing perceptions and attitudes of your company and system.

Mandate. Based on the worldview of the conviction, define what you must do in terms of a mission. This is your commitment to deliver value—relevance and differentiation—to the market.

Focused actions. Define the specific and detailed programs and tactics that follow from your conviction. These are the key themes and messages of your core strategy.

8. *Remember that tone and style are as important as substance* in driving an inside-out strategy. Remember these points:
   - *Touch.* Employee communications should be personal and intimate.
   - *Equip.* Arm employees with current facts and information.
   - *Involve.* Create an interactive dialogue that breeds employee ownership.
   - *Interest.* Communicate individually relevant, fun, and motivating messages to employees.
   - *Enlist.* Offer internal leaders a chance to become missionaries and storytellers.
   - *Persist.* Organize a 12-month planning calendar that includes all activities, briefings, meetings, and the two to four specific "touches" of each employee per year.

9. Needless to add, we believe that an important step in creating effective inside-out communications and a more productive organization is to *create an insurgent culture within your company.* You'll be communicating to all your employees that:
   - They are part of something big and important. It's not just a business plan; it's a revolution.
   - Every company objective is achievable—and *must* be achieved by "Election Day."
   - Every vote counts. Everything they say and do must result in moving votes in the right direction.
   - They must focus on moving the movable and define market targets according to attitude, with particular focus on the soft support segment in any group.
   - They must communicate and sell their own plans inside-out and enlist their group members first by transferring ownership of their strategies.

- They will be the ones who play offense in the market—they'll never allow themselves to be put on the defensive.
- They are learning how to win—and once they start winning, it's a feeling they'll never forget.

JUST DO IT

Communicate inside-out. If you get this right, nothing else matters.

- Sell your own employees before you try to sell anyone else.
- Overcommunicate key themes and messages.
- Communicate through friends and family.
- Define, overdeliver, and claim success.
- Monitor closely what your employees really believe.

Steps

- Translate ownership of your conviction and strategy to your employees.
- Communicate to these employees first.
- Remember, you can't make these inside-out communications too simple or repeat them too often.
- Drive communications through your industry's opinion leaders— or "big mouths"—and your friends and family.

Exercises

- Review existing research. Pull out employees' constructive ideas; find ways to fill the gaps between what these employees have and see today and what they want and imagine tomorrow.
- Do a strategic translation. Reduce your strategy to the simplicity of a 3 × 5 card. Write it down and keep simplifying it. And, on the other side, summarize your conviction statement. Then detail how this strategy and conviction can be communicated compellingly throughout your organization.

- Define your "Election Day." Refer to Chapter 1, "Adopt a Political Campaign Model" and define crisply and clearly an "Election Day" 12 months or more away, then map out a calendar of momentum objectives and proof points—opportunities to define, overdeliver, and celebrate your success.

- Commit to new employee research. Consider conducting new, cutting-edge research, either yourself or with assistance. This is an investment in your future success. So design a questionnaire as in Chapter 6, "Forget Reality: Perceptions Rule."

- Develop an actual program in which interested employees can "self-select," arming and ultimately asking employees for increasing loyalty and support. Write a plan for this program that includes an initial questionnaire, welcome letter, program description, competitive briefing, video, 3×5 card, executive stump speeches, success case studies, events, "work-out" sessions, formation of a "culture committee" of internal storytellers, and three to four "touches" of each participating employee per year.

- Repeat and repeat and repeat your strategic translation and core message. Keep repeating your strategy, your conviction, and the same focused, clear set of core messages for a minimum of 6 months.

- Create key databases and communications programs: A "big mouth" list of your industry's top 100 opinion makers and a "friends and family" list of your loyal employees, supporters, and friendly constituents. Launch a campaign to communicate with these groups at least every 2 or 3 months.

- Set up a War Room, an actual place wherein a talented campaign manager does nothing but think about executing your strategy every single day—and drives tactics with the urgency, focus, and aggressive discipline of a winning political campaign.

- Design a system to measure and monitor progress—to make necessary adjustments, reward success, and create momentum-building stories about what's working.

6

Forget Reality: Perceptions Rule

"Imagine what the audience thinks."
—Magician Tommy Wonder

- ➤ *Put yourself in the customer's shoes.*
- ➤ *Perceptions are reality.*
- ➤ *Invest in smart research.*
- ➤ *Win their hearts and minds.*

In the "reset" environment, the rules of leadership, business, and communications have changed completely. Today's consumers of information may be clients, employees, or investors, and they are empowered with instant and ubiquitous information. Consumers have infinitely more choices—and infinitely more information about how to make those choices. Brands have infinitely more competition. And all of us are inundated by a tsunami of information daily, the crassly trivial and the critically important swirling together in one crushing wave. Today, consumers of information feel overloaded.

Yet, at the same time, they compulsively seek even more information. They have more choices in the marketplace than ever before—yet they seek still more.

They are sophisticated and cynical consumers, and yet they are increasingly consumerist. They seek more information about every kind of decision, and yet they are buying on impulse more and on a bigger scale than ever.

Go figure. Better yet, go understand. If the world looks upside down, it's because you're looking at it the wrong way. This frustrating consumer behavior leads many marketers to shake their heads and say, "I just don't get it."

But this radically changed market behavior is completely "getable." You simply have to ask the right questions. And then (the hard part) you have to be willing to believe the answers. Most of the companies we work with have warehouses full of market data. But they still operate by anecdote: what the head of sales heard 15 years ago about the New England market, what the head of strategy thinks about people who go to Wal-Mart, what the CEO feels about CNN. That's why across most industries and companies today, greater and greater marketing investments are yielding lesser and lesser results. The old tried and true has been tried and just isn't true any more. Consumer perceptions and attitudes rule. They also change. And if you can't change with them, you're lost.

In fact, what managers think isn't very important in the great scheme of things. It's the customer, stupid.

- The great marketing innovator Joanna Jacobson once forced her entire sales force to put on T-shirts before entering the annual presentation of marketing strategy. In bold type on each of them were the words: "I'm NOT the target market."

Your marketplace reality is based on the perceptions and attitudes of customers and other key constituents. What they believe goes. You can try to shape their perceptions—it's doable, but it takes time and money. Or you can shape your strategy around their perceptions.

Forty years ago, in politics, President Lyndon Johnson famously discounted the value of trying to win an attitudinal war for public support of his Vietnam policies.

"Grab 'em by the balls," he said. "Their hearts and minds will follow."

Johnson was dead wrong. He and his successor Richard Nixon were forced to abandon the quest for victory in Southeast Asia because they had so badly lost the war for public support back home. They failed to calculate how much more effective it would be to grab people by their hearts and minds. And today, the Powell Doctrine has replaced Johnson's crass miscalculation: We'll never fight a war that doesn't have the support of the American people.

In Johnson's time, of course, ignoring the public was a little easier. It was, in fact, the norm in American politics. Once you were elected, you were pretty much free to do as you pleased. Now even the most powerful person in the world, the U.S. president, must essentially get his or her policies and programs elected every day. In this information age, every action is known or soon knowable. Today, the information revolution has empowered voters and consumers as a true force, not just on Election Day, but on any day when their attitudes are being polled or their chat rooms are abuzz or their purchase decisions are being tallied. Market information is instant—and consumers know it. They expect constant product and service improvement. If you don't provide it, they'll look for it somewhere else.

Individuals can make a very loud noise, and they know it. They can garner support and gather a crowd in a hurry. Today, Reagan's nickname, the Great Communicator, has become the president's job. The president must explain the complex working of the government to the American people. The president must gain consensus for his or her policies and for individuals in the administration. Further, the president must define the United States in the world—that is, must essentially communicate the American brand. And all this must be "elected" every day by voters, by the press, and by influentials all over the country and, increasingly, all over the world.

Of course, we believe in democracy (as the baseball player said, "It's been berry good to us"). However, all of us in Western culture have gotten more of it than we ever bargained for—the electronic democracy, instant, digital, and constant. The political conversations and market conversations are constant and flowing. As Richard Haas, president of the influential Council on Foreign Relations, has said, "The election is merely the culmination of the democratic process."

So, in today's business environment, you have to believe in marketing democracy. You have to treat all marketing communications as a two-way, interactive, and *living* conversation—inviting, carefully analyzing, and constantly responding in this dialogue. About 90 percent of marketers seem to be hard of hearing. Just look at their products, their customer relationship management, or their advertising. They're involved in a one-sided conversation. And, before long, they're just talking to themselves.

Without listening, this dialogue is impossible. Without constant, perceptive market research, effective strategy formation is impossible. The rate of change of perceptions and attitudes is getting faster and faster. The swings of national or market moods are getting more and more manic-depressive. The only choice in this environment is constant dialogue, the market conversation. It's ten o'clock. Do you know where your customers are?

Welcome to the age of the consumer. It's their world. And they know it. And we ignore this simple fact at our own peril.

In this chapter, then, we'll focus on understanding the power of perceptions and of establishing a core conversation that results in a productive customer relationship. In a world of change and market movement, we'll help you move ahead of the market.

SEE THE FUTURE—NOT JUST THE PAST

We believe in that core conversation. That's why we believe in research: It's often the best way to get into this dialogue. Research, particularly qualitative research, can be done informally as well as formally—just start asking questions and listen to the answers. This is where the best CEOs not only begin thinking about their future business challenges, but also monitor progress and learn about perceptual dangers and opportunities. It's what Tom Peters described as "managing by walking around and talking to people."

But what should you ask? In fact, the key to research is to ask the right questions—to develop points of inquiry that penetrate most deeply and attract and inspire the most relevant and useful answers. Even the most sophisticated researchers will begin their assignment by asking you, "What do you want to know?"

From our work in political campaigns and in helping to guide multimillion-dollar research for some of the world's biggest companies, great research begins with 10 great questions. Drawn from the insurgent principles in this book, these question areas will seem familiar to you by now:

- *What surrounds your customers' world?* In what context do they live? Overall, what are the most critical dynamics, forces, changes, products, services, and brands that touch them every day? How do they perceive that world?

- *How do they see the future?* Is it headed in the right or the wrong direction? Remember to ask your customers, again, the classic question that Ronald Reagan planted in the minds of voters to win the 1980 election: "Are you better off than you were 4 years ago?" What do they expect from your company or brand in the future? What do they expect from your competitors?

- *What do they dream about?* What is their *ideal* product, service, or offering in your category? In 1984, we worked with researcher Pat Caddell in developing his groundbreaking "Candidate Smith" research, which asked voters to construct their perfect, ideal candidate for president. In the business world, once you understand your customers' ideal product and service brands and brand relationships, you can probe ways to fill in the gaps.

- *What's in their hearts?* What emotional drivers are most important to your customers? Because more and more decisions are being made impulsively, more and more of marketing is driven by emotion. For example, in politics, one of the most telling measurements of any campaign is the degree to which people believe that a candidate "cares about people like me." Behind this question is a combination of curiosity and cynicism. "Can this person understand my life? And can I understand this person and the way she or he makes decisions?" They want to know the same thing from the companies and brands that they decide to deal with in the marketplace.

- *Where is their pain?* What are your customers missing that they most need? What do they worry about at night? For example, in the Internet gold rush, far too many companies were able to get funding, even though they were unable to answer the question of what specific marketplace pain their offering would address uniquely. Chances are those companies' stock certificates are about as valuable today as yesterday's newspaper.

- *What's relevant and different?* Value is created by relevant differentiation—by the benefits you provide to targeted customers and the way you provide them uniquely among all market choices. To achieve relevance, you've got to know what matters most to your customers. And, most importantly, you have to know what attributes communicate and prove differentiation for them. For example, we love to use a "laddering" technique that asks customers to rate a product's or service's most important attribute in order of importance to them. If you learn only one thing from market research, that one thing should be your target consumers' definition of relevance and differentiation in your market segment.

- *Are they movable?* What are your customers' attitudes toward your product, service, or company? Are they hard opposition?

Are they undecided? Are they soft support? In other words, ask your customers to tell you if they should be a prioritized marketing target. And get them to help you order your targeting priorities.

- *How can you overdeliver on their expectations?* What are your customers' current expectations based on today's market choices? What would constitute an overdelivery on these expectations? And when and how should you claim this success? In other words, as in Chapter 5, how can you best "DOCS" your customers—how can you clearly define expectations in line with their perceptions, overdeliver on them, and then remind customers of this success?

- *How can you best define yourself?* In the end, how must your customers see you? What must you stand for? How can you define your competition most advantageously? Ideally, positioning yourself effectively will result in positioning the competition as well. For a company, as for a political candidate, people are interested not only in what they decide to do, but in how they decide to do it. This tells consumers what they can expect from the candidate or company in the future.

- *Finally, how can you control the dialogue in your favor?* You must understand and objectively evaluate the effect of your competitors' claims in the marketplace. If they are the incumbent market leaders, chances are that they have control of the market dialogue. The question is, how can you take it away from them? What perceptual opportunities must be seized in order to turn consumers' attention to you? What core message and themes will help raise the ante in the marketplace?

To answer these questions, you can't simply rely on analyzing consumer behavioral data from the market or polling for current opinions. In fact, these techniques give you a very clear picture of what was—but not of what will be.

Most politicians understand this problem. Polling provides only a rearview mirror on the electorate. The political leader must have research that helps him or her understand what voters will think and how they will vote.

The market research you want will help you predict your targeted constituents' behavior in the future. Quantitative research is very important, but it must help set the future-market table, not just tell you what was and what is (which will be "what was" tomorrow). We use quantitative research to help define market segments and to do "presearch," testing hypotheses with our market targets: "What would you do, if . . .?"; "What would you think, if. . . ." We test a range of possible changes in our clients' products and services or the competition's products and services. We match hypothetical market concepts with variations in product formulation, channel, placement, and price.

Today, your business should use presearch to establish compass bearings within the reset environment—to dig deeply and pragmatically into customer perceptions into the future. Presearch is a powerful tool to help identify the most compelling and relevant set of customer strategies, themes, and messages into the next market.

Presearch can be conducted qualitatively or quantitatively. For example:

- *Qualitative focus groups.* This technique, developed in modern form by, among others, our colleague Dr. Ned Kennan, is based on group therapy techniques and methods used by the Mossad in debriefing Israeli intelligence agents as they return from spy missions.

  Focus groups involve a randomly selected, but purposely targeted, demographic group and a skilled and objective moderator.

  Focus groups measure the way a group interactively perceives, understands, interprets, and learns. They are particularly powerful in helping us understand the way in which new information moves a collective psychology, together, in discussion—as if this group sat around the same dinner table at which much of America pronounces products or causes "good" or "bad."

Warning: We won't forget the research we conducted several years ago for the Miller Brewing Company. After the initial results were favorable to Miller, we decided to experiment and instruct our moderators that the client was actually Budweiser and not Miller. Amazingly, this time, the results came out more favorably for Budweiser than for Miller—because the moderator kept leaning the focus groups in that direction. For years, we avoided doing market research in Japan because research companies were so anxious to please their clients with happy results. Just the facts, ma'am.

- *Qualitative in-depth interviews.* This research technique is similar to focus groups, but it utilizes an individual and one-on-one focus. These individual interviews are more convenient and flexible to arrange. Moreover, they often allow greater confidentiality, deeper probing, and higher-level contacts than focus groups. They are among the easiest and most helpful research methodologies that we use to get our bearings and establish initial strategic assumptions—to be tested more rigorously through quantitative research.

We also do in-depth research on specific consumer groups—for instance, what's called "anthropological" research, which delves deeply into key consumers' behaviors and beliefs—leading toward developing hypotheses to influence future behavior and beliefs.

FOLLOW THE LEADERS

We watch trend research to understand longer-term market effects. Of course, we realize that markets today seldom move in predictable cycles or patterns—they scuttle like spider crabs across a beach. But still, market effects can be understood. Lately, for example, many companies marketing to younger consumers have been enlisting the services of "cool hunters," who try to identify the first evidence of broader future trends. These researchers pay special attention to a group of market-leading consumers called "early adopters" (the innovative market researcher Nick Donatello has described a key group of over 30 million early adopters as "New Enthusiasts"). Early adopters are the most:

- Consumerist of all consumers.
- Self-confident of all consumers.
- Sensitive of all consumers to marketing messages.
- Cynical of all consumers in their reaction to those marketing messages.

Most importantly, the early adopters are constantly on the lookout for new concepts, products, or services. They're willing to try any new idea . . . at least once. And they particularly relish the role of leading other consumers to what they've found. Early adopters exist in every market, in every age and race and size or shape. They represent the "point of the wedge" for market development. And they can lead other consumers to a new idea—or stop it cold before others get a chance to try it.

During the last decade's economic boom, the numbers of consumers with early adopter attitudes and behavior increased greatly as more people gained confidence in their own shopping decisions (a combination of increased experience and increased information). These early adopters are closely followed by another group of consumers of significant size. We call them "progressive consumers" because of their very positive attitude toward new ideas, new choices, and change in the marketplace. What distinguishes these progressive consumers most significantly is that they are more influenced by the movement and personal communications of early adopters than by any other kind of communications.

Though early adopters and progressive consumers are constant shoppers, they're a very tough audience for most marketing communications. Their cynicism about marketing is partly a result of their saturation with marketing messages. But it's also about keeping their place at the head of the consumer line. When they see a product they've used in mass marketing, they consider it "over." And what early adopters want is anything but mass.

Progressive consumers want what early adopters want. And naturally, marketers want the early adopters and progressive consumers partly for their ability to sway the market, but also because this segment of consumers is significant in itself, as Donatello has shown. Importantly, early adopters and progressive consumers are much more concept- and value-sensitive than price-sensitive. Indeed, the sign of a product's success comes not only by reaching, but also by holding, early adopters with its ability to hold a premium price beyond its earliest market experience. That's what Starbucks has done so well—the fact that it's still getting over four bucks for a cup of coffee says that it's still holding its early adopter market, more than a decade after Starbucks was first discovered by these consumers.

So how do you manage marketing and brand communications with this tough audience?

What's most important to early adopters is the product itself. While they'll try anything, they are quite value conscious. They'll pay for true relevance and differentiation. But if their experience with the product doesn't live up to the brand promise, they drop it like a bad habit. This reveals a broader market trend among virtually all consumers: Not since the very beginning of mass marketing, more than five decades ago, has product quality and integrity been so important to so many. With vastly more choice and information, consumers are increasingly discriminating about product performance, particularly relative to product claims and imagery.

As a result, the next most powerful communications to early adopters are product distribution and placement. First, the product must not be too widely distributed in its introduction; this will spoil the early adopter's sense of discovery. Early adopters want to find new products as a part of retail concepts that they've also discovered. Again, mass is a turn-off. If a packaged goods product is introduced to create trial among early adopters, it must be seen in only the right places—and ideally it must be placed uniquely in these stores.

Next, package and label are key message channels for early adopters. They are looking for distinctive and intuitively useful packaging. That's often what draws their attention to the product in the first place. And early adopters and progressive consumers are diligent label readers. They want to see the "product narrative" on the label; they are looking for a unique character and values in the areas of development, manufacture, and ingredients. Of course, they favor brands run by entrepreneurial and obsessive owner/inventor/founders (like Steven Jobs of Apple or Jim Koch of Samuel Adams).

Moreover, early adopters and progressive consumers are very ad-unfriendly. They are very resistant to mass marketing. Even if they may enjoy television commercials, they're unlikely to allow the perception that they're moved by them.

A few years ago, studying young early adopters' reactions to new packaging for a product from The Coca-Cola Company, we did market interviews alongside the remarkable Canadian ethnologist Grant McCracken. It was 4 A.M. in Dallas, and we were talking to a young Indie Rock musician. He loved one of the new packages in particular. As he gazed at it admiringly, he admonished us: "Just . . . like . . . don't advertise it, okay?"

"Then how are we supposed to tell people about it?" we demanded.

"Just . . . like . . . leave me some bread crumbs, okay?"

That was the best advice anyone could give about marketing messages intended for early adopters or progressive consumers. Make them subtle, but clear. Connect the dots with integrated messages. Customize the appeal to the perceived relevance and differentiation defined by those very picky consumers.

GIVE THEM WHAT THEY WANT

What do today's customers want? What drives them? And, most important, how do you take advantage of their perceptions in order to serve them smarter, better, and more profitably?

Start with five critical perceptual axes along which a company, product, or brand must position itself to gain marketplace momentum today:

- First, there is *control.* For products from software to soda pop, from telephones to hamburgers, we find control to be an absolutely critical psychological need among today's consumers. After all, for over two decades, customers have been feeling a loss of control over their own lives—a loss of control over their time, their finances, their kids' education, their families' safety, their health care, the role of government, attacks from international terrorists. Current research shows that people want to regain control. They want to get hold of the reins again.

- Second, there is *customization.* For decades, the rule in manufacturing and marketing was optimization. Mass scale was what won in the wars and in the making and selling of products. The concept of optimization is to use the most limited possible technology to appeal to the broadest possible audience. The quintessential example of optimization in consumer products was the tube sock of the 1970s: "One size fits all." But 30 years of increasing market choices and information have convinced consumers to keep on searching for "that one size that fits just me." They expect to find products that will suit their needs and wants very specifically, and they're quite willing to keep searching until they find those products. Today, the insurgent marketing war is fought over customization—or even individualization. Customization, in Pascal's words, allows people to "teach themselves." It lets people feel that companies care about their own individual needs, wants, and dreams.

Today, companies are successful to the extent that they are able to focus mass technologies on smaller individual needs. Today, even a former optimizer like McDonald's will let you "have it your way": Specialized orders make up over 40 percent of McDonald's sales today. Verizon's customized calling plans are designed for the same purpose—the sense of control and customization, as much as the reality of those qualities.

Today, the age of optimization is over. Customization rules. Think about it in terms of one of the most successful products in marketing history: the Barbie Doll:

In the 1950s, there was the first Barbie—and it sold millions.

In the 1980s, there was "Ethnic Barbie"—and it sold hundreds of thousands.

In the 1990s, there came "Biker Barbie"—and it sold thousands as the total Barbie franchise grew by a remarkably large percentage.

And, in 2003, how close are we to "Personal Barbie"—to focusing on a single sale in a "Barbie of One" age?

- Third, there is *convenience*. In 1990, researcher Daniel Yankelovich found that 58 percent of consumers said that their life was too complicated; by the late 1990s, that figure had risen to 71 percent. What people want from marketing communications are guidance and navigation: "Tell me what it does for me. Tell me where to get it. Then get the hell out of my way." Time-pressed consumers don't just appreciate convenience; they demand it. And not just from products, but from product communications, too. It seems that there will always be at least one competitor who is willing to put its product between the consumer and your product, whatever it takes.

- Fourth, there is *choice*. Today, even with the seemingly infinite choice in every marketplace, consumers in every kind of

B2B or B2C product category are constantly looking for more choice. Providing choice within an existing brand family isn't easy, but it's totally necessary. That's what drives, for example, successful and constant new product development at Frito-Lay.

- Fifth, there is *change*. While authenticity is important to early adopters and progressive consumers, they still want to be refreshed; they still love change. When they reward a product or service with their loyalty, it's because that brand makes constant change and refreshment a part of its value proposition. These brands offer guidance and navigation through today's constant currents of change.

Remember, pigs fly—as long as your customers believe they do. It's their party. And we get into it only at *their* invitation. So we've got to be careful with that relationship and respectful of our customers' views.

In the past 30 years, around the world, we can honestly say that we know of no case in which voters have selected the wrong candidate—*based on the information they were given*. Losing an election does not mean that the voters got it wrong. It means, instead, that you failed to communicate your case to voters—or perhaps that you communicated your case, but they rejected it. The late Mo Udall had it right when he admitted the day after an especially painful election loss:

> The people have spoken—the bastards!
> —FORMER PRESIDENTIAL CANDIDATE MO UDALL

Sergio Zyman, former chief marketing officer at The Coca-Cola Company and all-around marketing genius, understands this as well as anyone in the world. He argues that today we must "smash open the black box of marketing" and get inside our customers' and prospective customers' heads. As he puts it, "You can never know too much about your consumers."

The first job of marketing, therefore, is not communicating well but rather listening well. It's about getting inside the heads of your audience.

Microsoft used to scoff at market research and marketing in general, claiming that product development was simply about a commitment to making "cool stuff." But, at the same time, the company has always devoted a hefty share of its total resources to its usability labs. These labs focus on how people use software, how they use PCs and other devices, how they work and think about work, how they decide on purchases, and so on. Invariably, Microsoft uses this competitive intelligence to find ways to get closer to its end users and to these consumers' needs and wants.

MANAGE PERCEPTIONS LIKE A MAGICIAN

Perceptions trump reality. For centuries, magicians have understood the power of their audiences' perceptions. In fact, their job depends upon perceptions overruling reality. Consider, for example, the world's greatest magicians and the perceptual principles that underpin their illusions:

- It's 1910, and arguably the world's greatest entertainer is instructing a packed house in Cleveland to take a breath along with him and hold it as he plunges into a bolted and locked 5-foot metal milk can filled to the brim with water. Harry Houdini is locked inside. His last breath is the audience's last breath. Now, a curtain is drawn around the spectacle. The seconds tick by. One by one, each spectator gives up and gasps for breath. One minute. Two minutes!! Three minutes!!! Soon a deadly nervousness descends. It spreads through the audience. There's panic. Houdini is drowning. Four minutes!!!! Get him out of there!

  What they didn't know was that the 36-year-old Houdini had escaped from the milk can 15 seconds into his deadly challenge. Sometimes turning newspaper pages rather too loudly, he would sit behind the curtain reading the sports section and waiting . . . waiting . . . waiting for near-hysteria to take hold beyond the curtain in the audience. Seconds before panicked spectators literally stormed the stage, Houdini reemerged from behind the curtain panting, wet, seemingly seconds from a drowning death—or so the audience perceived. Was it reality? Did they care?

- In 1983, did David Copperfield actually make the Statue of Liberty disappear? To this day, the spectators gathered to watch swear they saw him do it.

- In 2003, did David Blaine actually survive for 44 days in a glass box high above the Thames with no food and only water? That's what a skeptical British public watched—and that's what will no doubt be portrayed in the book and TV special to follow.

Magicians, good ones, are natural insurgent marketers. They live inside a world that considers only perceptions: *what the audience sees*. For them, this is reality. Houdini nearly died every time he escaped from the milk can. The Statute of Liberty actually vanished. Blaine defies the laws of nature. For centuries, in magic, perceptions have won out over reality. And today, in marketing as well, perceptions trump reality every time.

Let's look, for example, at three particular ways in which the world's greatest magicians think about perceptions—and fool us.

Perceptions Are Instantaneous

Recently, we sat with Max Maven, one of the world's top mentalists— a performer who uses a combination of psychology and theatrical techniques to approximate mind reading—as he repeated the mantra he uses to judge and improve his own and others' performances:

Within the first 30 seconds, you must answer for every audience three questions:

Who is this person?

What "story" are they trying to tell?

Why is it worth my time?

Thirty seconds. That's all the time we have.

Ten years ago, Fox News Channel's CEO and former client Roger Ailes wrote a book called *You Are the Message* in which he argued that we all make nearly instantaneous judgments about everyone we meet, based on their dress, looks, body language, charm, demeanor, and so on. It takes only seconds. Today, it probably takes less than 20 seconds. As television and the Web provide us with more and more imagery as a basis for comparison, we form quicker and quicker perceptions.

What is this?

What is it supposed to do for me?

Why do I care?

In entertainment, the world's best performers spend a lifetime getting ready to answer these three questions during the first minute of every show. They define themselves instantly. They know they must. And the fact that Ailes's FNC understands this better than anybody else is evidenced by its "out of nowhere" overtaking of CNN, the former incumbent.

Perceptions Are Reality

Remember the experiment conducted in law and journalism schools:

The instructor is lecturing, but suddenly something seems to be wrong. An intruder flings open the door and runs inside. The intruder calls out something. He or she creates instant havoc, then runs back out the door.

Immediately after that, the class is asked to record what just took place. An amazing thing happens: Nearly everyone disagrees about nearly everything that went on. Was the intruder a woman or a man? What did the intruder look like? How tall was this person?

How much did he or she weigh? What was he or she wearing? Did the person say something? Did the person do something? No two people agree—on any of it. *Everyone perceives something different.*

Recently, a similar psychological experiment was conducted on, of all the tough audiences, some of the world's best magicians.

They were asked to watch a film clip of two teams using two basketballs. The goal was to count the number of times one ball was passed between players of one team. Afterwards, they were asked if they noticed anything unusual in the film. Only *four* of the magicians saw it on first viewing. The vast majority did not. Most of the world's best magicians failed to notice a man dressed in a gorilla costume entering the picture partway, during the game, walking to the center, pausing and waving, and then exiting. The vast majority of magicians were looking for something else: the number of times a basketball was passed. Even for magicians, perceptions trump reality. Every time.

Max Maven (who saw the gorilla) reminds us of one of the most powerful tools that magicians, and marketers, apply every day. It's connected to something Pascal said 500 years ago. To paraphrase:

When a man teaches something to himself, the impact of that learning is far greater than if it is taught to him.

In other words, don't try to fool or trick your audience. People are too smart for that. Instead, let your audience, and your customers, trick themselves. Let them walk down their own individual "garden path"—don't try to take them there yourself. In fact, do what great magicians and marketers do constantly: Empower your audience to see it the way they want to. Allow them to make their own decisions and to draw their own conclusions.

In the 1970s, when the great illusionist Richiardi Jr. wanted to show that a wooden trunk was empty, it was unhelpful to simply tell the audience: "It's empty!" It was better, he knew, to take a large stick and slam it around the insides of the trunk with great speed and force to produce the convincingly loud and hollow sounds of total emptiness—there was no person, no lady, nothing hiding in that trunk.

In 1963, when Avis began to assume, brilliantly, an insurgent position against incumbent Hertz, it launched the "We Try Harder" campaign. Working with Doyle Dane and Bernbach, Avis staked out the "We Try Harder" position . . . but it did not completely define the details of what this meant for customers. In a sense, Avis empowered its customers, one at a time, to define what this meant to each and every one of them. And it allowed the momentum of perceptions to support its brand positioning: that the market "chaser" always tries a little harder than the market incumbent will. It was simply directing the existing perceptions of consumers. And it became one of the most successful marketing campaigns in history.

Magicians always do this. They call it, as world-class magician and producer Tony Clark explains, "misdirection." But, as he points out, "It's more accurately a matter of *direction*—directing an audience's perceptions where the magician can best take advantage of them."

In the 1940s, and for several decades to follow, Tony Slydini became one of the greatest sleight-of-hand performers that modern magic has ever seen. Even today, his adaptation of the very old principles of misdirection guide the strategies of the greatest magicians:

A bigger motion covers a smaller motion—and commands our perceptions.

Our body language and natural movement pull our eyes—and command our perceptions.

A "bait and switch" and the "off-beat" of an explanation—command our perceptions.

A "moment of surprise and revelation"—commands our perceptions.

A "meaningful statement" or, even better, a "penetrating question"—commands our perceptions.

Of course, we realize that no management of perceptions will overcome a poor product or service experience. "Nothing kills a bad product like good advertising," the great David Ogilvy once said. But it's important to learn how to communicate with consumers in the context of their personally held perceptions and attitudes.

In this sense, a magician's audience resembles a company's consumers and a campaign's voters. Always, perceptions trump reality.

Take another example: One of the world's greatest magicians, Jeff McBride, talks about the power of editing the audience's *memory*, as opposed to the reality, of a magical effect.

> As a magician pulls out the sealed envelope from his wallet, he says, "I don't want to touch it . . . you grab it . . . I don't want to touch it."
>
> Of course, the magician has been touching the envelope all along. But hours later, his words echo inside his audience's memories as they retell what they saw:
>
> "What was amazing was, he didn't even touch it!"

One more example: In the early 1900s, the bulldog-like, tough-talking Max Malini was the greatest performer of his day. And Malini stopped at nothing to get ahead of his audience's perceptions.

In Washington, D.C., he befriended a famous U.S. senator's tailor and convinced him to sew a particular playing card inside the lining of the senator's tuxedo jacket. Malini was preparing weeks, months, and even years ahead of the moment when he might run into the senator at a formal event. When he did, he would ask him to select a "forced" card, and then explain that the card had disappeared . . . only to reappear inside the lining of the senator's tuxedo jacket. Not surprisingly, the senator would perceive this as an impossible miracle.

Start with perceptions. Preparation comes before perceptions. And perceptions trump reality.

These great magicians know the power of getting ahead and staying ahead of perceptions—of what Tommy Wonder describes as "imagining what the audience thinks." They are similar to insurgent marketers. And they understand the power of putting yourself in the shoes of an audience, voter, or customer.

Perceptions Are Knowable

Additionally, great magicians recognize that they can learn and understand what an audience perceives—think of it as market research:

> In the 1940s and 1950s, one of the world's best mentalists, Dr. Jaks, was famous for hiding inside the men's room stall immediately after his performances—on the theory that in this facility he could best overhear his audience talking candidly about the show they'd just seen.

> More recently, Max Maven used to make an anonymous call to the theater in which he was playing, to ask: "Who was appearing? What did the guy actually do? And, by the way, was he any good?"

> Similarly, Jeff McBride describes what he calls the "point of inflection" and argues that magicians can't only practice before a mirror, because they will blink at the exact instant that a difficult sleight-of-hand move is required. In effect, it's a form of self-editing. We see what we want to see. And we can't depend on ourselves alone to watch what we do.

Magicians defeat the point of inflection by videotaping themselves and watching as if they were an audience. It helps them imagine what the audience thinks. And it helps them put themselves in the shoes of the people who watch them.

So, when it comes to perceptions, think like a magician. Imagine what the audience thinks—because, today, this is all that matters.

JUST DO IT

Forget reality: perceptions rule—and remember that moving today's consumers is harder than ever.

- Put yourself in the customer's shoes.
- Perceptions are reality.
- Invest in smart research.
- Win their hearts and minds.

Steps

- Define who you are—what you do and why people should care on your constituents' terms, not yours.
- Start with perceptions, and put yourself in your customers' shoes by investing in research.
- Give your customers more control, customization, convenience, choice, and change and you win.

Exercises

- Write a questionnaire and conduct your own qualitative research. As discussed, here are the 10 questions to ask your soft support customers or employees:

  What surrounds your world? What are the critical dynamics, forces, changes, products, services, and brands that touch you? How do you actually see the world today?

  How do you see the future? Is it headed in the right or the wrong direction? Are you better off today than you were last year or the year before? And why?

  What do you dream about? What is your ideal product, service, or offering?

  Where are your hearts? What emotional drivers are most important to you? And how can we prove that we actually care about and want to hear from people like you?

  Where is your pain? What is missing that you really need? What do you worry about at night?

  What's relevant and different? What matters most to you? And, importantly, what will prove difference to you? By priority, what attributes are most important and hardest to find?

Are you movable? How do you see our product, service, or company? How do you feel about us—are you supportive, neutral, or unsupportive?

How can we overdeliver on your expectations? What, in fact, are your current expectations? And what will it take to exceed them?

How can you best define yourself? Is our conviction compelling and credible to you? How do you see our strengths and weaknesses? And what about our competitors' strengths and weaknesses?

Finally, how can we control the dialogue in our favor? In other words, what message and theme make sense and even inspire you? And what subtle words, images, or actions are relevant, different, and credible to you?

7

Herd the Details: Remember, Everything Communicates

"I did not have sexual relations with that woman . . . Ms. Lewinsky."

—PRESIDENT BILL CLINTON

➢ *Everything communicates: Every detail is either adding or subtracting value; tiniest details make all the difference.*

➢ *If these tiny details are not working for you, they're working against you.*

➢ *Everything markets: Marketing is a part of everything you do.*

➢ *Brand is everything: Brands are the sum of everything you do.*

➢ *Brand is everybody: Everyone is part of your brand's meaning.*

➢ *It's not enough to just pay attention to details—you must make these details mean something, formed around one core communications strategy.*

It was October 1988. We were in a video studio somewhere in Hell's Kitchen in New York City with Michael Dukakis and his top campaign management. We were just there to watch, but even that was very painful. The campaign had reached that stage at which advertising was being created by committee—which means that the campaign was in full panic mode. At the moment, the committee in question was muzz-muzzing over a script that was being put together. It was developing a response, or rather a reaction, to the brilliant commercial done by Roger Ailes—if you were alive, you'll never forget the image: Michael Dukakis, with a silly smile on his face and a ridiculously ill-fitting helmet on his head, riding in an army tank. This would be our commander in chief? If a picture is worth a thousand words, in this case every one of these words was *loser*.

Somehow, we ended up alone with Governor Dukakis by the coffee machine. He asked what we thought of the response ad that his committee was crafting. In a towering moment of cowardice, we mumbled faint praise for whatever the hell the committee was getting ready to tape—30 seconds of high dudgeon attacking the attack as cheap politics.

"You know," Michael Dukakis admitted, "on the whole, I wish I'd never gotten into the tank."

In painful political moments like this, we have learned and relearned an indelible lesson: Everything communicates. And we have a lot of scar tissue to show for this education.

Politicians think of communications as speeches, press releases, bumper stickers, or television commercials. But in fact everything communicates: Every detail of what the candidate and the campaign say and do on or off camera communicates to some important audience. Nixon's sweaty brow in the Kennedy debates, Gary Hart's cruise on *Monkey Business,* Earl Butz's dirty jokes, Monica Lewinsky's blue Gap dress—all this will be remembered long after everything else about these politicos is forgotten.

It's the details that make the difference. Details define the politician—and, of course, as Howard Dean found out in the 2004 primary season, there are activists and enterprising journalists wait-

ing to pounce on every word. When Dean said that he hoped his candidacy would appeal to the "guys in the South with the Confederate
flag on their pickup trucks," he had to apologize not only to African-
American activists, but also to redneck pickup truck drivers. When
you lose control of the details, you're in trouble up to your belly button before you know it. You snooze; you lose.

To be sure, just about every campaign and every administration
has these moments of falling asleep at the wheel. And, suddenly,
they're hearing about it in Leno's or Letterman's monologue.

THE SMALLEST DETAIL COMMUNICATES

Of course, it's the same in business. Everything communicates.
Everything that you say and do is important in defining the value of
your brand and the success of your company. Unfortunately, you don't
have Leno and Letterman to call you on your mistakes; you often have
to wait for a couple of crappy quarters' numbers to wake up to the
problems that are seeping out in the tiny details of your operations
or communications: slightly bored and very irritable people representing you behind the counter, scuffed-up packaging on the shelf,
"for all other problems, press 9."

Think about it: Despite all the logo design, packaging development, advertising, and PR releases that you so carefully craft, what
really defines you in the marketplace?

Running for a plane through the Pittsburgh airport, we actually
saw a sign at a US Airways counter that read: "Closed for your convenience." And nothing we've ever seen better sums up the major airlines' service attitude. Yes, it was an accident—but almost any US
Airways frequent flyer might call it a Freudian slip.

A few months ago, we got a call about doing a quick brand marketing project with a well-known lawn mower company. But we knew
there was trouble the moment we pulled into the company's parking
lot and noticed the scruffy lawn and scraggly bushes in front of the
company's global headquarters.

Like you, we've spent a fair amount of time in corporate waiting rooms. Do you take a look around at the walls and dusty display shelves? Do you shuffle through the thumb-worn magazines on the coffee table? What does it all communicate? Most often, it reminds us that the cobbler's children have no shoes. So what exactly are *you* communicating in the details?

True market insurgents pay attention to these details, because, quite often, that's all they have to control—they have none of the big splash media or imagery of major brands. These true market insurgents agonize over the fine print on the back of the label. They put messages about quality on the inside of their bottle caps. They swarm all over customers in their showrooms. Most of all, they worry about the product—its quality and its integrity. Just walk the aisles of Whole Foods and look at the row after row of insurgent brands' communications.

McDonald's founder Ray Kroc was a famous stickler for nano-details. His motto for the level of operational discipline he expected from owner/operators was, "Clean the corners. The middle will take care of itself." That's why Kroc insisted that his franchisees be actively involved in their businesses: "You cannot buy a McDonald's restaurant as an investment; it's your main business or it's not your business." Even today, the average franchisee in the sprawling McDonald's system operates just three stores. And today's "back to basics" management under Mike Roberts will still drum an owner/operator out of the business for running a sloppy restaurant. God help you if a "mystery shop" turns up an overflowing wastebasket in the women's room.

Kroc instilled fanatical attention and an "everything communicates" microscopic focus on everything within the property lines, from the front counter to the far reaches of the property. He understood how important the little things are to customers, particularly at a restaurant.

Monica Boyles, a McDonald's veteran and keeper of the Kroc flame, tells the story of a trip with Kroc and several others in top management to check out the competition on a market visit. They ordered

everything the hamburger joint had to offer—all of them being careful not to taste too much. Then good soldier Monica started to gather up the leftovers and trash.

"What are you doing?" Kroc demanded.

"I'm going to throw this in the trash," she replied.

"Like hell you are!" he ranted. "Dump it in the parking lot!"

Leaving aside this story's environmental correctness, Kroc knew instinctively the positive and negative force of the "everything communicates" principle—that the trash would stay there for the rest of the weekend, crunching under car tires and turning off customers all the while.

Indeed, the smudge on your wineglass or the little brown speck on your silverware communicates volumes about what's going on in the kitchen of even the finest restaurant.

A few years ago, working for Continental Airlines, we learned the importance of "the coffee stain on the tray table." At the time, as market research showed us, the hidden, though constant, concern of the most frequent business travelers was safety—in fact, even with today's constant terrorist concerns, safety is an ever-present factor that drives more decisions than most airlines realize. Indeed, business travelers are often control freaks in their own work and don't particularly like the idea of locking the door to the cockpit, seeing this as a symbol of giving up that control. Multiply this factor by three or four for women business flyers—they really don't like the idea of two guys in the cockpit being in control of their destiny. And since few frequent travelers are themselves pilots or aircraft engineers, they must seek signs of security wherever they can find them. The oft-cited example: The coffee stain on the tray table leads to questioning whether the mechanics are tightening the bolts.

And it's true. One of the most disturbing signs for frequent business flyers is a grumpy cabin crew. This indicates strife within the airline—and that implies that mechanics and pilots have more on their mind than tightening the bolts and checking the in-flight digital displays. Interestingly, it's often veteran airline pilots who understand this issue best. From the outset, they communicate their own comfort and calm in any situation, as Tom Wolfe depicted so well in *The Right Stuff*. They'll drop unnecessary details into the perfunctory pilot's announcements when you reach cruising altitude. They'll pass on information from air traffic controllers. They'll predict to the minute how long you'll be bumping along in turbulence with the ice cubes jingling in your Scotch. In fact, these veteran pilots know that details are everything in their job. Taking care of those details is what their training is all about. And proving that they care about them makes the passengers feel a lot more comfortable about coming back to that airline. United Airlines still proudly broadcasts its pilots' communications with air traffic control on its in-flight entertainment programming.

Across industries, we've learned that businesses that have complex daily operational challenges—like airlines and daily newspapers, for instance—are often so consumed with these everyday challenges that the details of communications escape them. For them, trying to communicate one thing gets in the way of communicating another. For example, the federal airport security people are supposed to make us all feel safer as we go through the lines. But, in an effort to show political correctness, they assiduously avoid racial profiling—and often go overboard. Think about it: How much safer do you feel when you see them checking out a grandmother's sensible shoes or wand-searching a 5-year-old?

Okay, you get it. Details are important. Attention to detail is imperative in any business or any institution, team, or military unit. But how do you develop and maintain this discipline?

SHAPE DETAILS AROUND ONE CORE STRATEGY

It's probably the first rule of herding ducks—never lose your own sense of direction as you try to keep them waddling along. Details need direction. It's not enough to tell your people to care about the little things. It's not enough to impress them by citing examples of details that disconnect brand meaning. That's the *why* of communications discipline, but it's not enough. At some level, most employees already know that if you get the details of execution wrong, then everything else in your marketing strategy is for nothing. But today, you must constantly add the *what*. You must tell your people exactly *what* the details should be communicating:

- The most effective way to create a discipline for controlling the details of your company and brand is to form everything around one core communications strategy.

- We named our company Core Strategy Group to emphasize the importance of this central communications strategy—so that every client kept asking, "What's our core message to our customers? How are we communicating it? And how can we communicate it even better?"

Every successful political campaign develops a core strategy, formulated centrally by the campaign's core strategy group of candidate, campaign manager, issue experts, pollster/researcher, and communications consultants. This is the basic theme of the campaign, the fundamental answer to: "Why am I running?"

And the candidate and his or her campaign staff must answer this question in terms that are relevant to voters and that differentiate the candidate from the rest of the pack. In other words, political candidates create value for their crowded campaigns the same way products do on their crowded shelves.

Ronald Reagan, in the 1980 presidential campaign, could answer that question easily and compellingly: "I'm running to help get government off your back. I'm going to cut taxes to stimulate our economy. And I'm going to confront Soviet Communism to make the world safe for our kids and grandkids."

It was a simple answer, but it was very clear and was very clearly differentiated from the messages of his Republican primary opponents and the incumbent president, Jimmy Carter. Carter, indeed, was a fanatic on details, but all of them were discrete and disconnected from one another, adding up to—nothing. With the incumbent Carter himself failing to communicate what he stood for, the insurgent Reagan was able to position his opponent as supporting only an unacceptable status quo. And so the great majority of voters bought Reagan's simple core message. In fact, Republican or Democrat, we would argue that Reagan's three campaign objectives—get government off your back, cut taxes, and confront Soviet Communism—actually drove the activities of his presidency.

Everyone in the Reagan administration knew what his or her job was. And that's what your core message should do for you, too—inform your employees, stakeholders, and customers of what you do in terms of delivering relevant and differentiated benefits. This core message should tell every employee what he or she should be thinking about when he or she wakes up every morning.

Chances are, when somebody asks you, "What do you do?" you'll answer, "I'm senior VP of sales at Acme."

That would be like a politician answering, "Why are you running?" with, "I'm a Republican senator from Ohio."

It may tell them who you are, but it won't tell them why to vote for you.

- *Your company's core message must define who you are in terms of the relevant and differentiated benefits that you provide for all constituents.* This includes employees, shareholders, stakeholders, community leaders, customers, and prospective customers.

- *This core message should also provide some reasons why the relevant benefits should be believed.*

    "What do you do?" someone asks.

    "I work for Acme. We're the company that has developed the only really effective Road Runner traps on the market. Wile E. Coyote used our Acme Rocket to turn the Road Runner into road kill."

    This is your basic value proposition. Your core message doesn't just tell strangers what you do; it must tell everyone inside the company what they should do every day.

- *Your core communications strategy tells your people what's important.* It defines your commitment to deliver something meaningful and different to customers and to the community.

Be prepared for the next time you're buttonholed at a cocktail party or by your seatmate on an airplane and asked, "What do you do?"

Here's what we say: "We teach people to win, by teaching them how to think, plan, and act like an insurgent, not an incumbent—to be a true revolutionary."

DO AN "EVERYTHING COMMUNICATES" AUDIT

Your company's core communications strategy should connect to every other strategy in a hub-and-spoke relationship. And that core message should be drilled down to the tiniest details. Think about the customer's experience with your brand. Define it down to the smallest detail—for example, our client, Home Depot, lists the hundreds of "customer touch points" for every one of their stores.

Do an "everything communicates" audit of your company and your brand(s).

1. *This is about everything.* So include everything that your customer might come into contact with: every action, expression, interaction, and communication; every sight, smell, and sound.

2. *Think inside-out.* Start inside your own company and work outward toward the marketplace and then to usage and customer support.

3. *Think panoramically.* Try to include in the audit every word and every image, from first impressions to relationship management. Pay close attention to the product experience—every aspect of usage, from opening the package or accepting delivery to disposal or resale. It's one long brand communication—sometimes years long, sometimes lasting only a few seconds.

4. *Ask of every single thing in this audit: "What does this communicate?"* And ensure that no detail, no matter how seemingly trivial, escapes this strategic question and filter.

5. *Then ask: "How can we make it better communicate our core message?"* How can we make this help to communicate our basic value proposition? How can we align this detail better with our core strategy and message?

We're talking about your corporate letterhead, the way-finding signs in your company's offices, invoices, the way the phone is answered at headquarters, what you give as sales incentives, door handles, brochures and all other collateral materials, tags, dress code, what's in the refrigerator in the break rooms, users' manuals, and on and on and on. *Everything.* What does every detail say? What *should* it say?

For example, take Honda. Up until the early 1990s, automobiles were designed from the outside-in; they were styled first as sleek clay models, then as full-sized prototype wood or plastic body shells. As fuel efficiency become increasingly important, these models become smaller and more alike in their aerodynamics. At the same time, market research informed automakers that driver/owners basically couldn't tell one car from another. That's why Honda began a radical departure in car design: It began to design from the inside out—"driver first; machine second" was its guiding principle. And Honda realized that, unless the driver was sitting on the hood of the car, she or he had no idea how the car looked while she or he was driving it. By contrast, they could see an easy-to-reach, high-quality sound system, plenty of cup holders, and other driver-friendly and later kid-friendly (to keep the kids occupied and quiet on long trips) gadgets and gimmicks. Relevance and differentiation were communicated in every interior detail of Honda's new cars. Every single one communicated: "Honda."

EVERYTHING IS MARKETING

The textbook definition of marketing is "a process that adds value to transactions." But what exactly does your company do that's *not* intended to add value to transactions? Every aspect of your operations, administration, and communications should be adding value or it shouldn't be happening. Product development and manufacture is designed to add value, right? Recruiting, hiring, and managing talent should add value, right? Coffee breaks should add value, right?

The answer, of course, is yes. Everything should add value. And that's why everything is marketing. We realize that this statement will make a lot of people in your organization cringe. That's simply because they think of marketing as advertising and the big product blowups at trade shows. But you must expand their thinking. Marketing is everything. Everything that you do and say is either selling or unselling your value. If you care about your value, you sure as hell should care about marketing.

That's why the "everything communicates" audit is so important—because the details can unsell just as surely and effectively as the broad strokes can. For example, The Coca-Cola Company is one organization that traditionally has tried to add value to everything it does. In fact, the goal of everything the company does and says is refreshment; make it enriching, unique, uplifting. And when you think about the brand value of Coca-Cola, you think of the color red, the contour bottle, the Spencerian script, the polar bears, the refreshing product itself, the commanding retail presence, the self-serve fountains at fast-food restaurants, the co-branded signs, the advertising, the sponsorships, the trucks, Sundblum's Santa, the vending machines, and more. *Question:* What gives Coke its value as a product and as a brand? *Answer:* All of it. And any one piece of it—a discourteous Coke truck driver or a dirty can in the cooler of a convenience store—can undo all the rest, all the gazillions of dollars in manufacturing, distribution, and marketing.

Most companies' communications are peppered with disconnections and misdirections. Only the best companies arrange every detail in the same direction, communicating an effective message:

- If you say you're getting back to basics, why the lavish annual report? It may be because the people preparing it have no idea what your corporate strategy or brand meaning is all about. And these people may end up contradicting what your company is all about.

- McDonald's knows what a dirty bathroom implies about the kitchen. And Toshifumi Suzuki of Ito-Yokado, the owners of Southland's 7-Eleven, awoke his organization to the issue of dusty product on the shelf.

BUILDING BRAND IN MARKETING'S HOT ZONE

Today, the best retailers understand that it's not enough to have the right products in the right places on your shelves and in your display cases. You've got to create a total environment that is conducive to buying your products. In a world in which every industry, every mall, every shelf, and every medium is crowded with competition and every consumer's mind is cluttered with information, the point of decision has been moving closer and closer to the point of sale. We've cited Loblaw's research showing that about 80 percent of brand decisions in supermarkets are made at the shelf. And that rule is applying more and more to other retail categories. Consumers who are brimming with product information and shopping confidence—bolstered by the unending innovation of consumer debt managers—are making bigger and bigger purchases on impulse: huge plasma TVs, heavy appliances, furniture, automobiles, even condos and homes. "What the hell? Let's get it now."

As discussed, *the retail aisle is the "hot zone" of marketing today.* The whole cycle of awareness, consideration, and trial is happening there. For example, the great Stew Leonard created the most profitable retail square footage on the planet in his two dairy (plus, plus, plus) stores. While most food retailers were trying to direct their customers into a perimeter shopping pattern, forcing them to walk through the whole store to get to the basics of milk, eggs, and bread, Stew put the milk at the very front. But it was also at the very beginning of a nontraditional layout that works something like a salmon stream: a winding path through the store that's hard not to follow. While most food retailers were doing everything they could to reduce head count, Stew had more employees per customer than anybody else. And you would find these employees every few feet along that winding store pathway, handing out free samples, dressed up in costumes for the kiddies, and helping out in any way they could. Stew and Stew Jr. know how to control the environment in the hot zone of marketing today.

Just a few years ago, a mass marketer might hope to have the consumer walk into the store whistling the jingle from the TV commercial. Today, advertising can't outcommunicate the hot zone of retail. In the best case, when the advertising is seamlessly integrated with merchandising, packaging, promotion, and the product experience, the advertising probably plays in the consumer's mind when she or he reaches the shelf.

Marketing in the hot zone mitigates the advantage of mass—the solid walls of big-brand products are surrounded by the often more interesting concepts of the insurgent brands that elbow their way into the customer's attention. And, knowing that consumers want choice and variety, retailers give these insurgent ideas more opportunity than almost ever before. All this just increases the marketing heat. Product, product information, demonstrations, tastings, friendly ambiance, inviting smells and sounds—all this defines the hot zone. It's just details. And they're just everything.

- For example, look at Disney. Although they've faltered in recent years as competition caught up to their pioneering concepts, the Disney Stores revolutionized toy retailing by creating one of the first retail hot zones. Before their development, the driving concept in a toy store was to keep the merchandise away from the grabby little bastards. Toys were kept up high or behind glass. That cut down on breakage and "shrinkage" (stock walking out of the store in tiny coat pockets). But Disney turned this principle upside down. It arranged the toys so that they overflowed from display shelves and cases and tumbled out onto the floor. The stores encouraged kids to grab and play. Huge TV screens made sure that the kids related the toys to the animation fantasies that inspired them. Of course, Disney realized that the kids might be hard to detach from the toys they were playing with—but that would be the parents' problem. And it was, after all, a problem easily solved by Visa or MasterCard.

- Starbucks realized that drinking a four-dollar cup of coffee had better be a unique experience—so it created an experience to surround and envelop its customers. This included everything from overstuffed easy chairs to comfort food snacks to soft lighting to earth colors to wonderful roasting smells to its own line of background music—everything that helps make Starbucks much more than what's in the cup. And the experience is so memorable that it travels in the senses far beyond the store. The concept, by the way, was created from the enhanced memory of European coffeehouses.

  Starbucks does virtually no advertising. Instead, it uses distribution and discipline to provide quality products and an "everything communicates" attention to communicating its brand meaning in everything it does and everybody who does it. While other quick-service food concepts have seen their brand value diminished by the attitude and aptitude of their employees, Starbucks has trained workers to create meaningful differentiation. And by providing benefits like health insurance and profit sharing, the company has attracted and held better employees.

- Wal-Mart realized that its "stack 'em high, price 'em low, and watch 'em fly" concept would be light on customer support, so it put that support right at the very entrance to the store with its now famous geriatric "greeters." These folks not only provide a warm welcome, guidance, and direction, but also provide a contrast with the existing image of the discount store. And this is just one of the details that distinguishes Wal-Mart and has helped it dominate a sea of competition. Moreover, imitation is flattery. When Target Stores made the wise choice to change the dialogue and provide a differentiated concept in the discount space, it did so with details—cleaner store designs and merchandising, specific aspirational products and brands in each of the stores' categories—to help define the overall quality and overall shopping experience as a "cut above."

Everything markets. Everything is brand, and brand is everything. A brand, after all, is simply a frame inside which all of the impressions and interactions a consumer has with a product, service, company, or institution may be painted. These brand impressions are almost always pointillist paintings, created from the tiny dots of details. In the same way that most politicians don't understand that everything communicates, most managers don't understand that everything is brand. In fact, most managers tend to define brand as logo, labels, and advertising—marketing stuff.

And ad agencies are generally no better. They think of brand in terms of 30-second, carefully controlled images and messages. Even if their commercials are remembered (20 percent is considered successful day-after recall for TV commercials) and—an even slimmer chance—are believed (6 percent, remember, is the average credibility level for broadcast TV commercials), ad agencies still can't control the brand experience at the shelf. This, after all, is where competitive brands and concepts surround a product—and where the brand meaning comes to be associated with all sorts of impressions.

Indeed, we've sat through countless ad agency presentations in which the agency tells the client that the idea is to make consumers love the brand and then they'll use it. All the evidence, however, supports the reverse of this equation: If they use it long enough, they'll love the brand. And, if they use it often enough, the brand will take on highly personal meaning, an ideal meaning: the brand as part of the customer.

CREATE AN "EVERYTHING COMMUNICATES" BRAND STRATEGY

Once you accept the idea that everything is brand, you must develop a strategy and a tactical discipline to express the brand in every possible detail—in everything you do and say, in everything and everybody that has anything to do with the brand. Here's how to do it:

1. *Create a core communications strategy.* Answer the question, "What do we do?" And answer it in terms of relevant benefits that are differentiated from those of the competition.

2. *Define market targets.* Whom do you need in order to win the election? What are the gaps ("take what they give you!") that the competition provides?

3. *Create the product around the target consumer's wants and needs.* Don't just create a product—focus on a product experience.

4. *Define what your product experience means to your best customers.* Again, we call this "loyal voter" research. And we find that these loyal voters or hard supporters understand and can best express your product experience. They can, in fact, tell you how best to communicate their own rewarding and satisfying product experience to your other "softer" consumers.

5. *Describe how you will communicate active presence (usage by satisfied users), relevance (benefits of usage), differentiation, and credibility (fulfilling the implicit brand promise) in everything you do and say.* That is, work through Chapter 4's key brand dimensions.

6. *Define the way you will communicate a relevant and different (and therefore, valuable) product experience in everything you do and say.* Define customer "touch points," as Home Depot does. Create an enveloping experience around your product—even if all you have is a box or bottle or can on a shelf.

7. *Do a thorough "everything communicates" audit.* Get all your people to define how they're going to drive the details. And put everything you do and say—*everything*—through this strategic filter.

8. *Think from the product experience outward toward every expression, every piece of material, every meeting and show.* In other words, think virally—because it's the flow of day-to-day details and interactions that is critical in communicating, marketing, and building brand today.

In sum: "If you don't know where you're going, any road will take you there," goes the Buddhist saying. Strategy is your road map. And today, this map is going to be defined in the grainiest of details—these are the details that make or break brands and make or break value.

JUST DO IT

Herd the details: Remember, everything communicates.

- Everything communicates: every detail is either adding or subtracting value; the tiniest details make all the difference.
- And if these tiny details are not working for you, they're working against you.
- Everything markets: Marketing is a part of everything you do.
- Brand is everything: Brands are the sum of everything you do.
- Brand is everybody: Everyone in your organization is part of your brand's meaning.
- Herd the details around one core communications strategy—so everything communicates in the same direction.

Steps

- Understand that the tiniest details define success.
- Constantly police these details.
- Herd them around a core strategy.

- Keep translating your core strategy into a core message.
- Control every detail of your brand's definition.
- Win in marketing's "hot zone."

Exercises

- Preach "everything communicates" everywhere you go and raise organizational awareness. Never give a speech or presentation without making this argument.
- Refer to Chapter 5, "Communicate Inside-Out," and make sure that you've translated your core strategy and conviction into a core message. Pull out that 3×5 card and make sure that it answers these questions:

  Who are you?

  What do you do?

  Why should I care?

- Conduct an actual "everything communicates" audit and look at everything to ensure that every detail is reinforcing your core message, including:

  Internal and external research

  Employee cultural dynamics

  Organizational dynamics

  Internal communications tools

  Sales force materials

  Free media outreach

  Community programs

  Charity efforts

  Paid media

  Corporate identity communications

  Senior executive communications

  Operations

  Human resources

  Benefits and compensation

  Recruiting

  Investor relations

  And so on

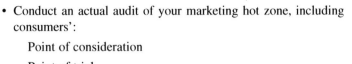

- Conduct an actual audit of your marketing hot zone, including consumers':

    Point of consideration

    Point of trial

    Point of purchase

    Point of consumption

    Point of reconsideration

    Point of retrial

    Point of repurchase

- Review the key brand dimensions in Chapter 4, "Play Offense," and commit to paper an everything communicates brand strategy defining:

    Brand destination and objectives

    Consumer needs and wants

    Intended product experience

    Brand presence, relevance, differentiation, credibility,

      and image associations

8

Deal with Crisis as SOP

"SNAFU: Situation Normal All F———- Up."
—ORGINATED BY U.S. MILITARY
DURING WORLD WAR II

➢ *Don't "manage" a crisis—solve it.*

➢ *Get control of the dialogue at the beginning of the crisis.*

➢ *Use the truth as the most powerful form of propaganda.*

➢ *Create a core strategy group that will keep your business focused and running while you're solving the crisis.*

➢ *Create a "crisis simulator" in your company.*

➢ *Play offense!*

When you say "crisis" down at the "Consultants' Union Hall" (Local 407), eyes brighten and heartbeats quicken. It creates a warm feeling all over the body, emanating from the general area of the wallet. Crisis jobs, it is said, are like tow-truck jobs: You'll pay anything to get out of the ditch. And these are truly great times for crisis and crisis consultants. These days, you can get sued for making hot coffee too hot. You can get sued for satisfying the hunger of the obese. You can get sued for suing people. Today, to put it simply, crisis is standard operating procedure (SOP).

The high-pressure, intensely scrutinized, every-second-counts atmosphere that used to happen once in a blue moon is now happening all the time. In fact, chances are there's a crisis brewing or boiling over right now in some aspect of your operations—and let's just hope you find out about it before you see it in the news. So, given the reality that crisis is SOP, we're going to teach you in this chapter to develop a crisis model that works every day and doesn't send your operations into a terror lock.

You'd better be ready for crisis. There are product crises, legal crises, financial crises, takeover crises, personnel crises, competitive crises, and discrimination and harassment crises, and there are crisis experts for every one of them. There are PR firms that are ready to deploy armies of crisis experts and law firms with legions of lawyers ready to fight on either side of a crisis.

All these legal and communications experts are trained in "crisis management." And that's just what they do: They manage crises— they don't solve them. Often, in fact, the tactics they push will prolong or even deepen the crisis.

A crisis itself is often less damaging than the companies' and individuals' reactions to it. It's the denial and cover-up that do the real damage. That's what brought down the presidency of Richard Nixon and the candidacy of Gary Hart and led to the impeachment of Bill Clinton. And today, in spite of these clear lessons of history, the first reaction of politicians seems to be the same: denial. The candidate's first press release denies the scurrilous charges, calling them a personal and partisan attack. A month later, there's the candidate's press conference, most often with his wife by his side, announcing his decision to enter the Betty Ford Clinic.

Corporate managers watch all this with a combination of amusement and disgust—and then make the same mistakes. The first reaction is denial. The second reaction is to stonewall—after all, the lawyers have told you that you can't say anything. Executive doors close. More lawyers are coursing through the waiting room—now, they're not even slowing down to announce their arrival. There are more double-top-secret meetings. And there's total radio silence from the executive floor.

"We've got to keep this quiet," the executives tell one another, but below the executive floor, they've created a firestorm of gossip. It couldn't be noisier. In the absence of hard information, people guess, with only imagination and anxiety to guide them. In the midst of all this, operations slow to a crawl, then grind to a halt. The idea of closed-door meetings in and around the CEO's office is to isolate the crisis. But, as a result of what's going on behind these doors, the crisis spreads like a virus through the company and its system of stakeholders.

- It's already too late. Whether it's in a campaign or an administration, we've learned in politics that a crisis creates a loss of control of the dialogue. And the only hope of regaining control of this dialogue comes at the very beginning of the crisis. After that, journalistic feeding frenzies and buffet tables of rumors and accusations take over. And there's only one way to regain control of the dialogue: Tell the truth. Fortunately, the truth is the most powerful form of propaganda known to mankind. The truth disarms both your friends and your enemies. It establishes you as the source of the next story and the next after that.

- Of course, the advantage of telling the truth is that the teller has control. But telling the truth well (the useful motto of advertising legend H. K. McCann's agency, McCann-Erickson, was "the truth well told") also means understanding the power of perception as truth (see Chapter 6). So, *you must not only communicate the facts as they are, but also communicate to the perceptions of your key audiences.* You must empathize with their feelings. And this simply means that when you tell the truth, tell it all and tell it fast, and, as the advice goes, you must also tell it to all audiences on *their* terms. It's not enough to be sorry if you're only sorry for yourself. You must recognize that the result of your actions has been the creation of disappointment and disillusionment; in reality, you've turned your own people into liars because they defended you.

- Stew Leonard, Jr., who runs the famous Stew Leonard's Dairy Stores in Connecticut, treats every instance of customer dissatisfaction as a crisis—and has created a model for dealing with crisis on any scale. When a customer brings a half-gallon of milk back to the store saying that it smells funny, the employee who opens it up to smell it is putting his or her job on the line. "No questions asked" is the policy, and Stew Junior enforces it strictly. At most stores, the manager will immediately open the milk, whiff it, and say, "Doesn't smell funny to me." At Stew Junior's, in contrast, the employee takes the milk back immediately and, importantly, doesn't just provide a replacement half-gallon in return. Instead, it's up to the employee to be creative and "oversolve" the customer's problem. For example, the employee may give the customer a half-gallon of ice cream to go along with the milk. "Think about it," Stew Junior says. "They took the milk home, cooked dinner, then opened the milk and found that it was spoiled. They're already inconvenienced and angry. Now, they've got to get in the car and bring it back to the store. All the way, their stomach is churning, because they're getting ready for a fight. It's up to us to make all that up to them." This "crisis response" is considered the everyday modus operandi at Stew Leonard's.

Our model for dealing with crisis drives lawyers crazy. When we're saying, "Tell the truth. Tell it all. Tell it fast," they're saying, "Tell nothing. Tell nobody. Tell it as slowly as possible." But our model is the opposite of "managing crisis." We want to *solve* the crisis. Our model for dealing with crisis is the famous Red Adair's Hellfighters—the guys who get the call to put out oil-well fires that are burning out of control. What they do is fly in, put out the fire, and fly out. The faster they do it, the more money they make.

That's the way it should be. Should somebody get more money for managing a crisis into the next fiscal year? Solve it. And you can solve most crises yourself, with your own internal resources. We're not, however, suggesting firing your law firm; in fact, we'd like to give you the names of some killer lawyers—because you're going to need the best of lawyers in these worst of times.

We recommend, in fact, that you create an organization that deals with crisis as SOP. And we recommend that you train for crises the way airline pilots do at Flight Safety. Train for every possibility. Develop scenarios that define the worst that can happen. And develop checklists of actions to take. Not only will this help you solve crises, it will also make your everyday actions and communications sharper.

What follows is our crisis checklist. You're going to see some very familiar ideas here—our objective is not to get creative with a crisis; it's to solve the crisis. So we apply the principles that work for all strategic situations, adapted for crisis:

1. *Solve the next crisis before it happens.* It's likely that 99 percent of airline pilots will go through their careers without losing an engine in flight. But for that one in a bazillion who sees that flashing light on the instrument panel and hears the blaring cyborg voice warning, the chances are very good that the pilot will say to him- or herself, "I've done this before—I know what to do." Redundant training for every kind of flying crisis is done in the simulator. And you can do this in your company. Assume, as airline pilot trainers do, that what can go wrong will go wrong—sometime. So create a core strategy group consisting of your executive team plus product experts, market researchers, corporate counsel, and communications managers. Create

a crisis simulator. Develop scenarios for product problems, competitive crises, regulatory or legal surprises, and on and on. Create specific checklists and call lists to be put into action immediately. Drill your executives on response communication techniques. Solve your next crisis before it happens. And, importantly, create a mind-set in that core strategy group: *You will not just survive the next crisis, you're going to turn it to your advantage.* You're going to win. Defense sucks. You're going to play offense.

2. *Count to ten—but not to eleven.* The point of training to solve crises before they happen is to keep the crisis situation from being unique—which means that the response will not be unique. This starts with a cool assessment of the situation. For example, PADI, one of the nation's top scuba-diving organizations, conducts state-of-the-art Rescue Diver training. In the course, the first thing you're taught is "SBTA": Stop, breathe, think, and act. Step back, remain cool, think, and work out solutions.

   In a business crisis, this means that you must begin by understanding what really happened. So get more than one view. Understand the crisis from 360 degrees. Understand the crisis's effect on all constituencies. And understand what must be done to solve the crisis with *each* constituency. Whether you can do it or not, and whether the lawyers think you can do it or not, you must know what it means to win—or the only thing your people can do is try to avoid losing, which is a very bad attitude in any situation. Define the win and plan to deliver it. To be sure, the demeanor of the core strategy group is going to spread. If your core team is panicked, the whole organization will feel it, as surely as a nervous horse senses a frightened rider. The reason to be cool is that you know what to do—you've done hundreds of hours in the crisis simulator. Stop, breathe, think, and act, and you're going to find a way to win. That keeps the whole organization, and the extended friends and family of the organization, cool and collected. And that can keep you in business.

3. *Segment your target constituents.* The principle of "move the movable" is even more important in the time-compressed situation of a crisis. There's only so much you can do under pressure and with the clock ticking. So you need to know who must be moved and who can be moved. Define the hard opposition, the soft opposition, the undecided, the soft support, and the hard support. And, as we suggested in Chapter 3, pay particular attention to the soft support. They're quiet and they're not a hundred percent behind you, but it's vitally important to activate them to support you—whatever it takes.

   The immediate challenge is to understand what it would take to solve the crisis for each attitudinal group. In the middle of crisis, we've often asked clients to make these assessments in the absence of attitudinal research, because of the crush of time. And we've found that salespeople, account management people, government relations people, investor relations people, and most others can do a very accurate job of this segmentation to develop action and communications priorities and to develop your core message.

4. *Form a core communications strategy.* Since you've accepted the principles of insurgent political strategy, you've already created a core messaging strategy for your company. And you won't throw that strategy away in a crisis—in fact, you should be able to simply expand upon it and drill down tactically on specific aspects of your core message for specific audiences' concerns. But if you try to manage a crisis without a strategy, you'll feel like you're playing goalie on a very bad hockey team. Pucks will be coming from every direction. And you'll be in constant defensive mode—which is exactly where you don't want

to be. Drill down to the details—remember, everything communicates, and in a crisis it's the details that communicate most vividly because of the increased scrutiny. And, importantly, it's contradiction and hypocrisy that create the press's favorite type of feeding frenzy. So don't let it happen. Be strategic—to the core. Then, your entire organization will speak and act with one message and one voice.

5. *Get control of the dialogue.* When you lose control of the dialogue, you're a pinball ricocheting off every wall and bumper. You're in constant reaction. It's like the worst of political campaigns—waking up every morning to check the overnight poll numbers and see what's on the Fox News Channel or in the *Times.* And, as we've said, the only time you can easily get control of the dialogue in a crisis is at the very beginning. And the only way you can easily get control is by using the truth as your tool. So, what we have learned in politics now applies to business as well: *What can be known will be known.* A telling example of this is the story of a certain Democratic candidate entering the 2004 presidential campaign, and actually floating this question with the press: "What's the statute of limitations on sexual indiscretion?"

In the 2003 California governor's race, Arnold Schwarzenegger learned that there is no statute of limitations. But he decided to trust the common sense of the voters. He told the truth … quickly. And the voters whacked the opposition and even the *Los Angeles Times* for breaking the story. Indeed, it wasn't that the charges of sexual play weren't true—candidate Schwarzenegger didn't deny them. The point was whether they were relevant.

Everything you ever did and everything your company ever did is in play. Dealing with this in the crisis simulator is a lot less painful than dealing with it under the hot lights of public accusation. Tell the truth: Define what you know, when you knew it, and what you're doing about it. When you do this, you take the ball away from your opponents. You get control of the dialogue. That means you will define the next and the next and the next moves. Of course, the lawyers will be apoplectic. So be it. If there's heat, take it sooner rather than get fried later. (Again, we'll suggest it: Email us and we'll give you the names of the world's best attorneys in terms of our principles.) Only the truth solves crises. Denial, stonewalling, and obfuscation "manage" the crisis—and usually manage only to get you into a deeper and deeper crisis.

6. *Communicate inside-out.* Because almost every crisis has potentially dire public consequences, there's a natural tendency to put the public fire out first. But you've got to start at the core of the crisis and focus first on your own internal audiences. After all, they're the ones that are most directly and profoundly affected by a crisis. Remember the message of Chapter 5: Get this right and nothing else matters. Get it wrong and your operations freeze up.

Again, if there was one winning aspect of Microsoft's long struggle with government regulators, it was the company's handling of its internal communications. Management was dedicated to the idea of protecting its people and its extended friends and family at all costs. And no company we've ever been around manages its human assets more seriously. Microsoft, for its part, wanted to make sure that its own people heard the news first and as often as possible. It made sure that its own people knew the arguments that the company and its managers were making publicly.

The sure thing in any crisis is that your employees will be besieged by their own families, their neighbors, industry peers, competitors, the press, and headhunters. You don't want them under attack and feeling defensive—or, worse, defenseless. For their sake, you want to make sure that they can argue your case effectively—that they can fend off the most boorish detractors—so you want them to have the same core communications strategy as you do. For your own sake, consider them as the most fundamentally important communications medium you've got.

We provide employees with the same 3 × 5 cards that we give to senior executives. This promotes the core concept of one message/one voice. Ever since the Vietnam debacle, when the standard dogface's answer to the reporters' question: "What are we doing here?" was "Beats the hell out of me," our armed forces have made sure that every fighting man and woman knows exactly what we're fighting for and what's at stake. The 9/11 terrorist attacks on America provided all the motivation needed for today's troops. "Freedom isn't free" has become an almost automatic refrain in response to the question: "Why are we in Iraq?"

So, if you do nothing else, you must develop your core communications strategy and execute it from the inside out. Anything else leaves you with a hollow core, a fatal weakness at the very center of your operations.

7. *Play offense.* Again, no major military or political victory has been achieved on the defensive. Until you get control of the dialogue and start playing offense, you will be losing, not winning. "Play offense!" was the battle cry of Bill and Hillary Clinton's White House MOD (Masters of Disaster) Squad with communications "Hellfighters" like Mark Fabiani, Mandy Grunwald, and Chris Lehane. Their trained instinct in any situation, no matter how challenging, was to find a way to get control of the dialogue and to get off the defensive. And when they seemed to be cornered, they'd attack. They'd often retaliate even before they were attacked. In fact, you can take any view of the Clinton

presidency that you want, but you have to admit to the precision of the political machinery.

Play offense:

- *Balance the picture.* Never allow an attack from the press or regulators or competitors to go unanswered. For example, market leaders like AT&T, McDonald's, and Coke gave their key competitors the freedom to attack constantly during the 1980s and 1990s. This was the equivalent of corporate "rope-a-dope." Rope-a-dope was Muhammad Ali's strategy of allowing his opponent to "punch himself out" while Ali covered up, leaning back, way back, on the ropes. Once the opponent tired of beating on Ali, the Champ would swing to the offensive. It seemed like a great concept at the time, but it probably contributed to the Great One's brain damage and subsequent Parkinson's disease.

  Today, corporations that allow detractors to attack without response are doing the same thing and suffering the same kind of damage. No attack should go without response. Anheuser-Busch, for example, has always taken every attack seriously. It has targeted seemingly insignificant competitors for ferocious—but truthful—attack. Anheuser-Busch believes that nothing is unimportant. And that's right. Respond to every attack.

  Furthermore, correct every single inaccuracy. The smallest incorrect detail takes on the force of fact as it is repeated and repeated by lazy journalists doing research in a media archive rather than developing their own basis of fact. For this level of attention to detail, we conjure up the image of NBA coach Phil Jackson disputing scores of seemingly insignificant rulings made by refs. He wants these refs to be aware that no mistake will be missed. The press, the regulatory authorities, and your competition should be aware of the same thing. Don't tread on me.

- *Speed wins.* We've emphasized the need to regain control of the dialogue at the very beginning of the crisis. And the imperative for speed never lets up during a crisis. So be the first to tell the whole truth. Be the first to define the context of a crisis, and others are likely to line up around your definition. In fact, this is what Clinton's team did so well: defining the "Affaire Lewinsky" as a personal, not a political or public, matter. And they did this faster than the other side. In football, the split-second issue of control of the line of scrimmage defines which team controls the entire 60-minute game. So don't just position yourself—position the opposition. Develop a bias for action and a need for speed.

- *Abandon subtlety.* Again, leave nothing to the imagination. In a crisis, subtlety leaves too much room for the opposition to maneuver. Speak clearly. Speak simply. And let your actions communicate as often as possible.

8. *Develop strategy for the "other side" of the crisis.* "Plan to win" is a useful cliché in a crisis. Winners plan, and only planners win. Develop a core strategy for the crisis—but also develop a strategy for what you'll do when you win. Develop a "postcrisis" strategy. Turn your company's focus from "right this minute" to the future, but don't try to erase the memory of the crisis. Instead, use it to create a new learning and a new attitude. In our experience, this "crisis-as-SOP" culture creates the Bear Bryant ideal of a team that is "mobile, agile, and hostile." Be smarter and tougher, but continue the core strategy that got you to the other side of the crisis—and, importantly, don't make any changes that change the fundamental meaning of your company and your brand among your most important constituents.

9. *Keep in touch with reality.* Though timely research is often difficult to achieve in a crisis situation, make sure to keep a sense of dialogue going with your key audiences. Perhaps the most damaging aspect of a crisis is the bunker mentality. The isolation created by sudden change and challenge can lead to enormous mistakes. So make attitudinal research a launching pad for as many actions as possible. And make sure that strategic researchers are part of your core strategy group and a constant influence on what you do and say.

The whole idea of the insurgent model of strategy and actions is to get to the "win." Therefore, you must define the win that you want and the discrete successes on the way to that win that you can reasonably achieve—in other words, "do the doable." Veterans of political campaigns will tell you that the campaign atmosphere is one of constant crisis. But the best campaigns are also an example of constant progress toward an ultimate goal. And that's an atmosphere you'd probably love to have inside your own company. So don't treat a crisis like a unique event—because today, it will be your business's day-to-day reality. Be ready and be prepared for crisis in everything you do.

JUST DO IT

Deal with crisis as SOP. Let the new reality trip up the competition, not you.

- Don't "manage" a crisis—*solve* it.
- Get control of the dialogue at the beginning of the crisis.
- Use the truth as the most powerful form of propaganda.
- Create a core strategy group that will keep your business focused and running while you're solving the crisis.
- Create a "crisis simulator" in your company.
- Play offense!

Steps

- Recognize that today crisis is SOP.
- Create a core strategy group and a crisis plan.
- Create a "crisis simulator" and a checklist.
- Train for crisis and train to preempt crisis.
- When crisis comes, use truth as the most powerful propaganda.
- Train to treat every customer interaction as a potential crisis.

Exercises

- Train SBTA—stop, breathe, think, and act—inside your culture. And empower your employees to overservice dissatisfied customers who are "in crisis"—who bring even the smallest problems to your employees.
- Form a core strategy group—including your executive team, product experts, researchers, corporate counsel, and communications managers—and have this group prepare a crisis manual that includes 24/7 contact protocols and information and a crisis checklist.
- Use this crisis checklist to conduct frequent simulations and drills. The crisis checklist and simulation outline should look like this:

  1. *Assess all realities.*

     Legal

     Communications

     Financial

     Technical

     Political

     Regulatory

     Media

     Customer

     Employee

  2. *Determine crisis objectives.*

     Collect facts; check facts; disseminate facts.

     Speak with one company voice.

     Control the situation, limit damage, and protect the company's reputation.

3. *Form a strategic checklist.*

   Be disciplined and cool.

   Form a crisis plan.

   Control the dialogue.

   Remember that truth is the best propaganda.

   Communicate inside-out throughout your organization.

   Play offense; don't just react.

   Centralize crisis operations within your facility.

   Think through scenarios.

   Invest in the "post-crisis" period.

   Monitor crisis realities.

4. *Form a simple message.*

   It should have two or three key points.

5. *Form a situation room.*

6. *Plan key tactics.*

   Create an internal statement:

   - What did we know?
   - When did we know it?
   - What are we doing about it?

   Create an internal timeline.

   Create internal Q&As.

   Review media to be contacted.

   Review web-site communications.

   Segment and target constituents by attitude: hard opposition, soft opposition, undecided, soft support, and hard support.

   Update "friends and family" and "big mouth" lists.

7. *Review media protocols.*

   Before and during a crisis, a clear plan should be prepared to determine the following:

   - Who will be authorized to speak to the press?
   - Where and how frequently should press briefings be held?
   - Where should the press congregate?
   - How will information be coordinated with police and law enforcement if necessary?

9

Rebels with a Cause

Who are today's insurgents? Which companies best model the rules of insurgency and embody the underdog advantage?

We've nominated 10 candidates: Rebels with a Cause. Each has a passion for playing offense, for controlling the dialogue, for riding ahead of the forces of change, and for taking advantage of nontraditional marketing strategies and communications tactics.

Five of these Rebels with a Cause—Starbucks, Jet Blue, Krispy Kreme, Nokia, and Red Hat (Linux)—are public with a combined market capitalization in excess of $100 billion. One company—Mobile One—recently went public; one company—Ben & Jerry's—is a subsidiary of Unilever; and three companies—Google, Patagonia, and Red Bull—remain private. Importantly, while each insurgent company is very different, all 10 enjoy impressive growth and profitability trajectories. All 10 are helping define the future of their respective industries.

Below we review these 10 Rebels with a Cause and identify many of the insurgent behaviors they exhibit to create and maintain their underdog advantage.

BEN & JERRY'S

One of the most unusual insurgent stories in recent American business history is Ben & Jerry's,[1] a Vermont-based manufacturer of superpremium ice cream, frozen yogurt, and sorbet. Founded in 1978 in a renovated gas station in Burlington, Vermont, by childhood friends Ben Cohen and Jerry Greenfield with a $12,000 investment, Ben & Jerry's now boasts over $450 million in annual revenues and 750 employees. Made from Vermont dairy products and high-quality natural ingredients, Ben & Jerry's ice cream is distributed in 46 states, and the company has 87 franchised scoop shops, 4 company-owned stores, and an increasingly global presence.

The Profile of an Insurgent: *Ben & Jerry's*

Established:	1978
Founders:	Ben Cohen, Jerry Greenfield
Products:	Superpremium ice cream, frozen yogurt, sorbet
Competing Products:	Häagen-Dazs
	Dreyer's
Parent Company:	Unilever (as of 2000)

STEPS TO VICTORY

Making a Difference

From the very beginning, Ben and Jerry embraced a number of insurgency's most basic tenets, recognizing that a huge number of consumers were disenchanted with a "business-as-usual" approach—they were starved for genuineness, social responsibility, and imagination. When Ben and Jerry surveyed the landscape of the competition, they saw sameness, predictability, and subpar standards. The two founders set out immediately to find the best, healthiest ingredients; embrace the community with social programs; contribute to charities even when their volume was unimpressive; and design every aspect of their business using models of corporate social responsibility—many of which they pioneered and are now SOP in many American corporations. To succeed, Ben and Jerry had to be different, and they were *very* different. Their methods have always been highly unconventional. In 1986, for example, they launched the "Cowmobile," a mobile home designed to carry huge volumes of ice cream and distribute free scoops across the country. Ben and Jerry even drove the mobile home and scooped the ice cream themselves! But, 4 months into the trip, the Cowmobile burned to the ground in Cleveland; thankfully, no one was injured. Ben's quote, cited around the country, was that it "looked like the world's largest baked Alaska." He was thinking about promotion even in the face of disaster—always thinking and communicating like an insurgent.

Crafting a New Market

The $20 billion U.S. market for ice cream, by far the world's largest, is very competitive and aggressive and has traditionally been dominated by "dynasties" such as Dreyer's and Nestlé. Based on supermarket statistics in 2001, ice cream volume sales by quality segment were superpremium, 3.5 percent; premium, 51.5 percent; and regular, 45 percent.[2]

Ben & Jerry's targeted the most competitive and relatively new segment, superpremium ice cream. This category was, in effect, "invented" by Pillsbury, which, in the late 1970s and early 1980s, had adopted its own insurgent strategy of creating a market where there was none—of taking what they give you. As Al Ries and Jack Trout contend in their book *Positioning and the 22 Immutable Laws of Marketing*, you need to own a defined brand in the mind of the consumer—so if you can't own a position, you must "create a new category" that you can claim ownership of. That is precisely what Häagen-Dazs did, using a European name, expensive, rich ingredients, and a pint size (as opposed to the standard gallon and half-gallon sizes). And Häagen-Dazs was an instant sensation. Predictably, many pretenders to the throne tried to imitate this success, challenging Häagen-Dazs—unsuccessfully, until Ben & Jerry's came along. Ultimately, Ben & Jerry's reinvented the space by creating a super-premium ice cream with a social conscience.

Points of Difference

With so much competition, Ben and Jerry decided to take a slow, incremental approach to growth—differentiating their growth approach and strategy immediately. They understood that since they had no resources for acquisitions or mergers, and very little revenue for large-scale advertising campaigns, they had to set themselves apart. They had to quickly stake out an undefined territory and maintain that position with constant innovation, freshness, and consistency. Given the amount of sameness, hype, and spin associated with mass merchandising, and with consumers weary of simply being told what to think and feel about purchases, Ben & Jerry's leapt out immediately from the pack. Their difference: Ice cream that is at once "real," natural and innovative. So Ben & Jerry's regularly marched out wild, exotic flavors such as Cherry Garcia, named after the legendary Grateful Dead guitarist, who, incidentally, has millions of dedicated fans the world over. Instantly, brilliantly, they created a niche market. Other offbeat flavors followed, including Chunky Monkey, with bananas and walnuts, a flavor suggested by a New Hampshire college student. As a consistent insurgent, Ben & Jerry's has always found ways to remain fresh, new, and unpredictable.

Ben & Jerry's Timeline

1963	Ben and Jerry meet in gym class on Long Island
1978	Open for business in a gas station
1981	First franchise in Shelburne, Vermont

1984	B&J sues Pillsbury
1987	Cherry Garcia flavor debuts
1992	Sales hit $131 million
1997	B&J in Japan, Holland, France
2000	Unilever buys B&J for $326 million

Cultural Icon

Modern pop culture enthusiastically embraced Ben & Jerry's wild desserts from the beginning, and the company has managed consistently, with guerrilla-fighter-like efficiency, to appear in mainstream media free of charge. In 1990, for example, David Letterman cited the 10 least popular Ben & Jerry's flavors, including "Zsa Zsa Gaboreo" and "Norieggnog." So, by the beginning of the 1990s, its quirky, unconventional mannerisms had made Ben & Jerry's a cultural icon. Even the company's mainstream quest for a corporate CEO, in 1994, reflected its consistently unconventional approach—the company took out nationwide ads for a 100-word essay contest to create a job description for the new leader (in addition to retaining a search firm). First prize was the job of running the $150 million corporation; second prize was a lifetime supply of Ben & Jerry's ice cream! Eventually, former McKinsey & Co. partner Robert Holland was hired through the search firm, but he wrote a poem to stay within the spirit of things.

Duels with the Incumbent

Ben & Jerry's challenged the incumbents, such as Häagen-Dazs, head on in true "David and Goliath" style. Its very first commercial employed a simple jingle that said: "There ain't no Häagen, there ain't no Dazs, but there are two real guys named Ben and Jerry!" Faith Popcorn, the futurist and consultant on consumer trends, best characterized this approach as a "real sell, delivering a real message in a real way." As diehard idealists who refused to compromise, Ben and Jerry vigorously identified themselves as "hippie capitalists," wedded to their values and unabashedly flaunting them in every manner possible. Moreover, they stated up front that their goal was to help make the world a better place in every phase of their operation. All their products, for example, had to be "natural" or organic, with no hormones or artificial ingredients, and all of their suppliers had to meet the same rigorous standards. Furthermore, Ben & Jerry's supported, through a foundation, programs to address a range of social and environmental problems facing the world.

Initially a curiosity, this altruistic approach was soon grabbed onto by the press, which extolled its virtues and helped launch the company as a "vanguard of responsible capitalism." Headlining even nonbusiness sections of the national press, Ben & Jerry's "crossed over" into lifestyle and mainstream news columns. It deployed unconventionality and countercultural expressions, in many ways nontraditional and even anticorporate, with great gusto and result. Perhaps *Megatrends 2000*'s author John Naisbitt summed it up best when he cited Ben & Jerry's as "most certainly . . . the new model of the corporate form that we will see created in the twenty-first century."

Accolades and Acquisition

As a result of its consistent, unwavering support for social causes Ben & Jerry's has received numerous awards. These include the Corporate Giving Award from the Council on Economic Priorities in 1988 and the U.S. Small Business Persons of the Year, presented by President Reagan in a White House Rose Garden ceremony the same year. Ben wore an Italian waiter's jacket and Jerry wore the only suit he owned. Ten years later, in a Harris poll of 1100 Americans, Ben & Jerry's was chosen as one of the top 20 "really good" companies in the United States. Similarly, in a New York University Stern Business School study, Ben & Jerry's ranked fifth among the top 20 "most reputable companies in the United States" and led in the Social Responsibility category. Finally, in 1999, an episode of *Everybody Loves Raymond* showed the characters touring the Ben & Jerry's factory—for the entire show. The rewards of unconventional, insurgent marketing.

In 2000, the Anglo-Dutch corporation Unilever acquired Ben & Jerry's for $326 million ($43.60 per share for 8.4 million outstanding shares). Ben and Jerry negotiated a unique deal that ensured that they, in collaboration with Unilever, would work to build an even bigger ice cream business—with global ambitions and based on the socially responsible values that launched and defined their brand. That year, a parade of hot air balloon tours, toe-wrestling contests, and a flowing pipeline of maniacal odd flavors ensued—and the insurgent beat goes on to this day.

Notes

1. www.benjerrys.com.
2. www.infores.com/public/us/about/iri/default.htm.

GOOGLE

Throughout the world, Google has become an indispensable tool for Internet users. Though a latecomer in the 1990s dot-com boom, the company managed to overtake some of its well-established competitors through a combination of innovative technology, persistent drive, and impressively nontraditional marketing. Google has established a reputation for being the best—and the number of current users offers a daily testament to how well its reputation has spread.

On the surface, Google's story is the classic dot-com rags-to-riches tale: Two graduate students successfully commercialize a revolutionary new product. But most industry observers agree that Google represents a unique case of start-up success. In fact, Google went from underdog to big dog through carefully designed insurgent strategies, allowing it to take control of the search-engine market dialogue and translate that into success. In every way possible, the company projects the simple, effective image of the search engine that has won it so many accolades in its few short years of existence; from technological innovator to web-site designer to upper-level manager, everybody is either a "Googler" or "Googling." And this insurgent success has left Microsoft and the investment community itching to jump onto the Internet express that is Google.

The Profile of an Insurgent:
Google

Corporate Facts*

Launch Date:	1998
Number of Employees:	> 1000
Estimated Revenue:	$30–$500 million
Estimated Worth:	$15–$25 billion[†]
Monthly Users:	73.5 million
Web Pages Indexed:	About 3 billion
Languages:	35 (results)
	88 (interfaces)
Services:	Advertising
	Internet search

Management

CEO:	Eric E. Schmidt, Ph.D.
Founders:	Sergey Brin
	Larry Page

Growth in Numbers

Daily Queries[‡]

1998:	10,000
02/1999:	500,000
12/1999:	3,000,000
6/2000:	18,000,000

12/2000:	60,000,000
02/2001:	100,000,000
Present:	200,000,000

Awards

Larry Page and Sergey Brin, the company's founders, were both named MIT's youth innovators to watch.

*Source: Company web site, www.google.com.
†Various sources.
‡Figures are approximate, source: company web site, www.google.com.

DORM ROOM INSURGENTS

The Early Years

In 1998, when Larry Page and Sergey Brin brought Google from their Stanford dorm rooms to the global marketplace, they created an entirely new style of Internet searching. Focusing solely on speed and relevancy of search, the two founders incorporated several unique features into their operation. For example, Google's search-engine technology is notably different from its competitors' because it lists search results based on a web page's popularity. In other words, Google first locates a query on as many web pages as it can, then evaluates each page's relevance based on the number of links that lead to that page. Google, moreover, has obtained a patent for this technology, which it calls PageRank. Furthermore, Google gives no preference to advertisers in its ranking upon the return of results—a practice that has discredited many other web sites.[1]

Becoming a Verb

The name Google is a play on words with the noun *googol*, which is a 1 followed by 100 zeros.[2] Now, with Google's soaring popularity, the company name has become a common dictionary reference in its own right. As the *Economist* points out, "If the ultimate measure of impact is to have one's name become a new verb in the world's main languages, Google has reason to be proud."[3] To "Google," in fact, has taken on a meaning beyond that of simply running an Internet search: It's a dating tool. Many first-time suitors will Google people that they are considering relationships with to find out more about them on the Web. And the growth rate of "Googling" has been astounding (see the information on user growth in the sidebar).

The company prides itself on relentlessly pursuing faster searches. For example, its technical gurus have managed to reduce the average search time from 3 seconds in 1999 to 0.2 seconds in 2003, claiming that it is inefficient for users to have to wait longer.[4] This focus on speed has helped create a large, loyal user base. And today, Google's nearly 70 million loyal customers run between 150 and 200 million daily searches.[5]

More importantly, not only has Google become an online search engine leader, it is also leading the way in Internet advertising—an industry that has been struggling of late. Google links advertisements to the key words in a search, in what has become known as "targeted advertising." Essentially, the company runs a continuous online auction to sell its ads to the highest bidders, in what has become a very successful model called AdSense. Moreover, Google licenses its patented search technology, called PageRank, to many other companies; it is now quite common to see web pages powered or enhanced by Google. So, in 5 years, Google has managed to become the world's most popular search engine and create a revolution in Internet advertising: This insurgent has left its incumbent competitors wondering what hit them.

Spurning Microsoft and the IPO Debate: Google Today

Google remains a privately held company, primarily controlled by its founding designers and leading venture capitalists. In 2003, Google firmly rejected takeover advances from Microsoft and continues to remain stubbornly out of the public investor marketplace. Some industry experts predict that in time, Google will succumb to the same fate as Netscape and Apple in the face of an onslaught from the Microsoft behemoth. In the near future, however, many investors are eager for their chance to become part owners of the estimated $15 billion firm.[6]

It is widely speculated that their chance could come as early as 2004, perhaps through an Internet auction,[7] in what would probably be one of the most significant dot-com IPOs since Netscape. According to some, "Google is likely to be as important a company as eBay and Microsoft, and that's really saying something."[8]

SEARCHING FOR COMPETITION

Yahoo!

While Yahoo! has fallen prey to the Google insurgency, the company clearly plans to make significant inroads into Google territory. Yahoo! remains Google's most important competitor, controlling just over 25 percent of the market.[9] Although Yahoo! has been licensing its search technology from Google since 2000, acquisitions of AltaVista, Inktomi, and several smaller search engines are helping position Yahoo! for a comeback. Moreover, Yahoo! is more diverse than Google, offering free email services, among other things, and also owns the Overture search service, which operates an advertising-targeting service similar to Google's.[10] Furthermore, the company is significantly larger than Google, with 2002 revenues totaling nearly $1 billion, after a year of negative earnings in 2001.[11]

The Rest

Other important search engines include America Online (AOL) and the Microsoft Network (MSN); however, big as they are, neither company represents a threat comparable to that of Yahoo!. Together with Yahoo! and Google, these companies round out what many call the "Big Four" in search engines.[12] AOL, which controls about 20 percent of the market when combined with other Time Warner companies, currently uses

Google search software to power its own Internet portal. Meanwhile, MSN attracts about 17 percent of all web queries.[13] Neither company seems especially poised to take aim at Google.

FEELING MORE THAN LUCKY: THE GOOGLE DIFFERENCE

Simple Focus Breeds Loyalty: Word of Mouth Does the Trick

Google's focus on speed and relevance is its trademark. Everything at the company revolves around it. According to Urs Holzle, a Google engineer, "We have only one product. . . . That's search. We don't show people things that they aren't interested in because, in the long term, that will kill your business."[14] Perhaps the most compelling evidence of Google's drive for simplicity is its own web site: There are only 37 words on the entire page. No distractions; no elaborate graphics that could hinder download time—just the search engine.

This inner drive and disciplined focus are at the core of creating the Google that so many web surfers have come to love. How loyal are Google early adopters and users? Well, for one thing, they are Google's biggest advertisers. The company, in fact, has acquired a 40 percent share of all online searchers without spending a dime on advertising; instead, it relies on the word-of-mouth encouragement of its hard support base to attract new Googlers.[15] In addition, "Google uses its loyal users [hard support] in a way almost no other Internet company does, to improve and extend its product. For instance, the company gives outside developers free access to its code. To most companies, that's anathema—but to Google, it is a way of expanding its use into areas that the company itself might never have imagined. Hence the collection of games and toys devised by geeks, based on Google's search technology."[16] (See other examples of strategic open sourcing by Linux and Matsushita elsewhere in this book.)

Diverse Revenue Streams: What Makes "AdSense"?

Today, Google has successfully maintained a balance between its core operations and its search for profits. In fact, in diversifying revenue streams, Google actually adds to its almost fanatical focus on its search-engine operations, for it uses the same technology that runs its queries to customize its advertising sales. Moreover, Google makes its technology available to power other web sites' search functions as well (see "Simple Focus Breeds Loyalty"). Interestingly, Google's innovative advertising revenue stream has been creating waves in the Internet industry, as many consider online ads to have lost their profitability following the dot-com bust in 2000. In fact, the Internet marketing revolution propelled by Google and, to a lesser extent, Yahoo! (a Google partner and competitor at the same time) has created a $1.5 billion industry that is projected by some to more than quadruple in size in the next 4 years.[17]

Here's how the AdSense program, as Google labels it, works: Google uses its search-engine technology to link advertisements to the query topic. The system is designed to make the advertisements more relevant to searchers, thus increasing the likelihood that they will "click through." Moreover, irrelevant or underused ads are eventually dropped from the Google site. So the focus is on a relevance that is integral to Google's core operations, and this focus on relevance is reinforced through the company's advertising innovation. Furthermore, the product line extension, in combination with technology licensing and a huge set of loyal users, has made Google into "a company that makes real money."[18]

Recently, Google has also engaged in buying up some rival ad-targeting programs.[19] However, this effort represents just one more step in Google's effort to maintain control of the Internet search industry dialogue. According the *Economist*, "All told, 75% of referrals to websites now originate from Google's algorithms. That is power."[20]

To Google and Beyond

Google faces several challenges as it enters its sixth year of operations. A possible IPO in 2004 will come at a time when the company faces renewed competition: On the one side, from Microsoft, and on the other side, from reinvigorated efforts by former and now surpassed rivals such as Yahoo! and AOL. Moreover, critics have questioned whether the Internet advertising revolution will continue to strengthen; while others are quick to point out that without any other features besides its central search engine, Google is susceptible to simple consumer loss at the hands of its competitors. Nonetheless, Google remains confident that it can withstand the competition by maintaining focus. One thing is for sure: This household insurgent has made waves in the Internet community and is digging in for the long haul—knowing that, in many ways, it must remain the underdog.

Notes

1. Richard Thomson, "Google Sweeps Search Engine World," *Evening Standard (UK),* April 18, 2003. Evening Standard, 2003.
2. www.google.com.
3. "The Economist: Where Is Google Headed?" Oct. 30, 2003. Economist Business Intelligence Unit Ltd., 2003.
4. Thomson, "Google Sweeps Search Engine World."
5. Ibid.
6. Jeremy Warnar, "Outlook: Googling All the Way to the Bank as Microsoft Squares Up," *The Independent,* Nov. 1, 2003. Independent Newspapers (UK) Limited, 2003.
7. Leslie Walker, "To Place Ads, Google Searches for Best Bidders," *Washington Post,* Oct. 30, 2003. The Washington Post Company, 2003.
8. Kevin Maney, "It's a Fact: Google May Scratch the High-Tech World's 9-Year IPO Itch," *USA Today,* Nov. 5, 2003. Bell & Howell Information and Learning Company, 2003.
9. Verne Kopytuff, "Google's Future Looking Good/ Bulked Up Search Firm Beats Up Rivals," *San Francisco Chronicle,* Nov. 9, 2003. Bell & Howell Information and Learning Company, 2003.
10. "The Economist: Where Is Google Headed?"
11. Yahoo! 2002 annual report, www.yahoo.com.
12. Ben Elgin and John Cady, "Sharpen Your Internet Search; All Search Engines Are Not Equal. Knowing Where and How to Make Your Queries Can Help You Avoid Ads and Get Exactly the Information You Want—Fast," *Business Week,* Nov. 3, 2003. McGraw-Hill, Inc., 2003.
13. Kopytuff, "Google's Future Looking Good."
14. Thomson, "Google Sweeps Search Engine World."
15. Richard Siklos, "City-Midtown View-Ubiquitous? Omniscient? It Must Be Google," *Sunday Telegraph,* Nov. 2, 2003. Telegraph Group Limited, London, 2003.
16. Thomson, "Google Sweeps Search Engine World."
17. Walker, "To Place Ads, Google Searches for Best Bidders."
18. Thomson, "Google Sweeps Search Engine World."
19. Walker, "To Place Ads, Google Searches for Best Bidders."
20. "The Economist: Where Is Google Headed?"

JET BLUE

On his second birthday, David Neeleman saw a tiny red airplane on his cake and knew that aviation would someday define his life. Thus was set in motion one of the most successful stories in airline history. As an entrepreneur out of college, Neeleman eventually launched Morris

Air, based in Salt Lake City, Utah, and then, in 1993, sold it to a company that has taught us many insurgent lessons: Southwest Airlines.

Morris Air was a successful regional experiment—a "proof of concept" that a low-cost, high-quality airline could succeed.

Interestingly, Neeleman's involvement in the industry's nuts and bolts knew no bounds; he was the inventor of "Open Skies," an e-ticketing system that the industry quickly embraced. Open Skies was purchased by Hewlett-Packard in 1998. And Neeleman parlayed these and other successes into a dramatic leap on February 11, 2000, with the launch of Jet Blue. Neeleman funded the venture with $130 million in capital from investors such as Weston Presidio Capital, George Soros, and Chase Capital. In fact, this was the highest capitalization of any airline launch in history, and Neeleman, who told the world he was going to "bring humanity back into air travel," has not looked back since.

The Profile of an Insurgent:
Jet Blue Airlines

Established:	2000
Founder:	David Neeleman
Cities Served:	22
Ticket Price Range:	$59–299
Revenues 2000:	$104 million
Revenues 2002:	$635 million
Profit 2002:	$95 million
Major Carrier Losses 2002:	$7 billion

TAKING OFF

Thin Air Up There

Most "low-cost" airlines are launched with a shoestring budget, an aging fleet of planes, a "no frills" and "cattle-car" concept, and a lot of prayers.

At the other end of the spectrum, mainstream airlines have been operating in the red for years. World airline operations lost $10 billion in 2001 and nearly $7 billion in 2002[1]—and a projected $5 billion this year.[2] This, then, is not a business for the faint of heart. Former Department of Transportation Assistant Secretary Patrick Murphy, who initially granted Jet Blue space at Kennedy Airport, makes this point: "I keep a book on my coffee table called *Deregulation Knockouts,* and about 82 airlines came and went in the first ten years of deregulation . . . like New York Air and Air Florida."[3] In this context, in September 2002, Jet Blue stunned the business world with its 6-month performance report: 500,000 passengers, 4,328 flights, 99.9 percent completion factor, 80.25 percent on-time ratio—and its first month of profitability!

Soaring Higher: The Jet Blue Difference

Brand-new planes, Airbus A320s, outfitted with all-leather seats; 24 channels of free Direct TV for every passenger; plenty of legroom; uniforms designed by Stan Herman, president of the Council of Fashion Designers of America, featuring a midnight-blue, Prada-like look; superlative customer service; no lines; and a youthful, hip, classy, innovative ambiance at every phase of operations—this all set Jet Blue apart from day one. Fares range from $70 to $199, for example, from New York to Orlando—with fares to Los Angeles from New York *starting* at $99. Moreover, the dreaded "advance purchase" and "Saturday night stay" have been jettisoned, resulting in legions of business travelers who were fed up with the larger carriers' $2000 price tag for round-trip coach tickets from coast to coast, and budget fares that were laden with restrictions and requirements flocking to the airline. For once, hype met expectation—and even exceeded it. Flying actually is fun again—and with more than one added edge: The JFK hub, housed comfortably in the former United Airlines terminal, features Deep Blue, a stylish sushi bar, and many other amenities. "We were starved for an airline like this," says Christopher Hayes, the chief investment officer at Rulison & Co., a financial firm based in Rochester, New York. Hayes, who has lately forgone his frequent-flyer perks on rival US Airways, has already flown the newcomer 12 times: "It's hard to compare flying Jet Blue to other airlines."[4] For the weary traveler, then, Jet Blue is a revelation, the "anti-airline," providing almost everything the other airlines do not. Airline travel has been forever transformed.

2002 AWARDS AND ACCOLADES

Best Domestic Airline	*Condé Nast Traveler,* 2002 Reader's Choice Awards
Best Domestic Airline— Coach	*Condé Nast Traveler,* 2002 Business Travel Awards
Best Domestic Airline— Value for Cost	*Condé Nast Traveler,* 2002 Business Travel Awards
Best Domestic Airline	North American Travel Journalists Association, Five-Star Award
#2 Domestic Airline	*Travel and Leisure,* 2002 World's Best Awards
Best Low-Cost Carrier (Runner-Up)	*Business Traveler,* 2002 Best in Business Travel Awards
"It" Airline	*Entertainment Weekly,* 2002 It List
Editor's Choice	*Worth*
Airline of the Year	*Airfinance Journal*
Americas Corporate Finance Deal of the Year	*Airfinance Journal*
Marketer of the Year	*Advertising Age*
Finance Award	*Airline Business,* 2002 Airline Strategy Awards
Best IPO of 2002	Corporate Finance Magazine

Aerodynamic Business Model

Jet Blue has a very basic business model:

- *Start with a lot of money.* Jet Blue is the best-capitalized air-line start-up in history. This means that it was able to invest in the best product available. And you see this in its new planes, comfy leather seats, free satellite TV, and fast check-in technology. So when unexpected downturns occur, such as rising fuel costs or 9/11, this extra cash is the best insurance policy.

- *Fly new planes.* Jet Blue's fleet of new Airbus A320s comes with a host of advantages. New aircraft are more reliable, so they spend less time on the ground, where they don't make money. Plus, they're more efficient, so they spend less on fuel than other carriers. In fact, the youngest fleet in the skies belongs to Jet Blue.

- *Hire the best people.* Jet Blue screens employees rigorously and trains them well—while providing them with the best tools. This means that its people are motivated and service-oriented. And they love changing the industry for the better! It's what gets them out of bed in the morning.

- *Focus on service.* Jet Blue finds that because it offers customers the best experience it can deliver, most customers come back regularly and tell their friends and family about the airline. It's not rocket science—customers have given Jet Blue incredible word-of-mouth recommendations. And this is viral marketing at its best.[5]

Jet Blue purchases only one type of aircraft, keeping maintenance costs down and eliminating the "penny-wise, pound-foolish" attitude of other start-up airlines that bought all kinds of different used planes and then paid for this with increased repair costs and customer discontent. Moreover, Jet Blue's flight attendants, many of whom answered ads in *The Village Voice* and *LA Weekly*, pitch in between flights to clean up—another cost saver and key factor in quick flight turnaround times. In fact, the company focused immediately on younger, better-educated, hipper flight attendants just out of college. These recruits, who were not necessarily looking for a career, but rather were looking for an exciting interlude in their life's journey, soon became eager, motivated workers. And this focus has paid off with awards, rave reviews, and enormously high levels of customer satisfaction.

Contrary Cost Flight Plans

"Despite the focus on cost, Jet Blue has expenses that most other airlines have rejected. It has configured its planes with emergency equipment such as life rafts and beacons for flying over water, thus allowing its flights to swing out over the ocean to avoid congestion on crowded East Coast routes. It has worked closely with controllers to 'tunnel' to its upstate New York destinations. That means flying at 10,000 ft., rather than the usual altitudes above 18,000 ft., which enables Jet Blue to avoid traffic jams in the air lanes."[6] "It costs us about $400 more per flight," says Chris Collins, vice president of operations. "But getting to your destination early is priceless."[7]

Routes to Success

Low-cost airlines, such as Midway Airlines in Chicago, generally operate out of regional hubs, and their expansion and profitability are often problematic. In 1978, airline deregulation had one major flaw for start-ups: LaGuardia and JFK in New York, O'Hare in Chicago, and National Airport in Washington, D.C., were exempt from the deregulation, rendering it nearly impossible for start-ups to break into the profitable, incumbent-controlled markets in those cities. Additionally, in spite of the low-cost airlines' proliferation, none had offered a full range of flights around the country out of New York City. Those that had made it to New York were serving area airports, not the main hubs of JFK and LaGuardia, and were offering only regional service.

With a serious interest in the airline industry—and his own personal experience with overpaying for short commuter flights from New York to Albany during his campaign—New York Senator Charles Schumer found Neeleman both promising and engaging. So Senator Schumer helped Jet Blue with the federal approvals necessary to acquire a place in a major hub, JFK.[8] Schumer's comments were telling: "I was looking at why upstate New York was not gaining jobs the way the rest of America was. After interviewing companies and people all over, I found that miserable air service was one of the reasons. I saw it myself: When you run for office, you have to fly to Buffalo, Rochester, Syracuse, and Albany. You call up, and they charge an outlandish fee for a round-trip ticket. You'd think that by paying $600 or $700 for a ticket, you'd be getting a beautiful plane, a beautiful seat. Instead, you'd get to the airport, and you were at the tail end of some terminal. Then, they made you walk downstairs onto the tarmac to a little propeller plane. On a nice day, they gave you peanuts."[9]

Neeleman articulated the importance of New York as his core market, saying, "It's No. 1 in retail sales, you have this large population that makes a lot of money per capita and everyone in New York would like to get out. At the same time, everyone outside New York would like to come in. It's truly the nirvana of all markets."[10]

The first two flights for Jet Blue were from JFK to Albany and JFK to Orlando.

FLYING HIGHER AND LONGER

The Future of Jet Blue

Jet Blue has learned many lessons from the consistently successful industry insurgent: Southwest Airlines.

Today, as the United States's most profitable airline, with a growing base of committed customers eager to get on its flights, Jet Blue is in an ideal position to continue its growth and success trajectory. Currently, there are plans to build a $1 billion Jet Blue terminal at JFK, a project supported by business executives, city officials, and private partnerships. This terminal will have 26 gates and occupy 1.5 million square feet.[11]

Jet Blue plans to become the largest domestic carrier at JFK, with over 200 flights a day by 2009. Preservationists, however, are challenging the plan because of its "intrusion" into the landmark TWA terminal, which is directly adjacent to the development plans. They object to the apparent demise of this terminal at the hands of such an upstart. This TWA terminal—with sweeping views of the same tarmac where "society" types sipped cocktails and watched planes come and go—is a monument to travel's "glory days" in the 1950s and 1960s.

Jet Blue's response has been to design around this TWA terminal—in effect, to enclose the old terminal with architectural and functional designs that will allow the new insurgent to encase the old incumbent in a symbolic, respectful embrace.

Notes

1. http://www.travelbiz.com.au/articles/c9/0c00c7c9.asp.
2. http://www.aardvarktravel.net/chat/viewtopic.php?t=2179.
3. Alex Williams, "Superfly," *New York Magazine*, Jan. 31, 2000, http://www.newyork-metro.com/nymetro/news/biz/features/1879/.
4. *Time* magazine, July 30, 2001.
5. Jetblue.com.
6. *Time* magazine, July 30, 2001.
7. Ibid.
8. *New York Magazine*, Jan. 31, 2001.
9. Ibid.
10. Ibid.
11. *New York Observer*, Aug. 4, 2003, p. 1.

KRISPY KREME DOUGHNUTS

Dunkin' Donuts, take notice: In each of the last 3 years, Krispy Kreme has doubled its profits, leading to a quadrupling of its share price.[1] Producing nearly three billion doughnuts annually, Krispy Kreme has emerged as a perennial favorite on Wall Street, outperforming almost all major indices since it went public at the turn of the century. With the company performance as hot as its doughnuts, Krispy Kreme is rapidly expanding throughout the United States and around the world. Fueled by word-of-mouth advertising and a cultlike clientele obsessed with the "original hot glazed" doughnut, the company is characterized by its operational simplicity, customer orientation, and incredible brand focus. It is not uncommon for hundreds of people to line up in anticipation of the opening of a local Krispy Kreme; after all, the company has a policy of having only one establishment in a given area to maintain scarcity and brand image.

The Profile of an Insurgent:
Krispy Kreme

Facts and Figures

Net Income (2002):	$33.5 million
Sales (2002):	$491.5 million
Stores (2003):	335
Employees (2003):	3913
Countries Served:	4 (U.S., Canada, U.K., Australia)
Daily Doughnut Production	7.5 million
CEO:	Scott A. Livengood
Founded:	1937
IPO:	2001
NYSE symbol:	KKD
Headquarters:	Winston-Salem, North Carolina

Awards

2003, 2002: Platinum Award for customer satisfaction in Restaurants and Institutions' "Choice in Chains" ranking in the category of Doughnuts/Cookies/Coffee

All information from company web site.

KRISPY KREME HISTORY

From Neighborhood Store to Stock Market Darling

Founded in 1937 by Vernon Rudolph in the small town of Winston-Salem, North Carolina, Krispy Kreme tries to continue to have a local feel.[2] The founder initially began by selling doughnuts to grocery stores, but quickly switched to selling hot doughnuts directly to customers. In the 1940s and 1950s, the company began to spread gradually throughout the southeastern United States, but most of the stores were still run by families. Krispy Kreme became concerned about the variance in the quality of the doughnuts sold by its different establishments, and thus, during this time period, it perfected a method of delivering identical dough to each store and equipping the stores with a standardized set of doughnut-baking machinery. Beatrice Foods acquired Krispy Kreme in the late 1970s, but a small group of the original founding family repurchased the company in 1982. In the mid-1990s, the company began planning for a far-reaching expansion outside its home market in the southeast. Aided by a loyal following of customers dedicated to "hot doughnuts now," Krispy Kreme began to grow rapidly. Its stores are generally rather large because the company puts its baking process on display (though recently smaller stores have been designed for the most popular areas of large cities). By the time the first store was opened in New York City in 1996, the company's growth was gaining national attention, and in 2000 Krispy Kreme held a successful IPO.[3] Today, "Krispy Kreme is perhaps the only company that can announce the opening of five stores and make national news."[4] Other aspects of the Krispy Kreme business model include doughnut delivery and, more recently, corporate partnering.

A Hole New World: Krispy Kreme Global Dreams

The rapidly expanding company opened its first international store in Canada in late 2001. Since then, the company has expanded to Europe and Australia. Krispy Kreme opened its first British store in 2003, with at least 25 more expected to open throughout the United Kingdom in the next 5 years. While there is some debate about whether foreign tastes offer enough support for a doughnut market, the company appears to be initially satisfied with its overseas development and has its sights set on Japan, South Korea, and Mexico as well.[5]

DIETARY RESISTANCE AND DUNKIN' DOMINATION

While no one really considers doughnuts to be a healthy treat, most health experts agree that this snack food leans toward the very unhealthy. For example, Krispy Kreme's doughnuts often have anywhere between 12 and 21 grams of fat, up to a third of the total mass of the doughnut.[6] Unsurprisingly, the doughnut industry in general—and Krispy Kreme doughnuts in particular—has come under intense scrutiny by dietary and health organizations.

The doughnut market is extremely competitive. In the United States, the competitiveness is a function of the sheer number of doughnut stores, while abroad the sector is competitive because of the smaller size of the market. Regional doughnut chains such as California-based Winchell's Donut House and Rhode Island–based Bess Eaton Coffee Shop & Bakery are generally slightly smaller than Krispy Kreme and have actually been using this insurgent company as a model for their own operations.[7] While these companies often have a significant presence in their niche markets, they are often left in Krispy Kreme's shadow. On the national level, Tim Horton's and Dunkin' Donuts hold 29 and 54 percent, respectively, of the overall market share, compared to Krispy Kreme's 12 percent share.[8] The company also purports to compete with companies such as Starbucks and Einstein Brothers Bagels and with local supermarkets.[9]

The Big Doughnuts

Tim Horton's, while younger than both Krispy Kreme and Dunkin' Donuts, has the advantage of having merged with Wendy's Corporation in 1995. This Canadian company has several unique offerings, including a frequently available 24-hour drive-through option. However, it is clearly better known in Canada than in the United States.

Dunkin' Donuts, owned by Allied Domecq, is clearly the doughnut king. Its 5700 stores (though not all are stand-alone) dwarf the several hundred owned by Krispy Kreme. Nonetheless, in 2001, Dunkin' Donuts began to take notice of the underdog from North Carolina. When Krispy Kreme signaled its intention to expand into the Boston area, Dunkin' Donuts' home market, the move generated a "tremendous amount of discussion"[10] among executives at the giant doughnut firm, even though Dunkin' Donuts had more stores in Boston alone than Krispy Kreme had in the whole country.

Dunkin' Donuts is an enormous challenge for the insurgent Krispy Kreme. With nearly $3 billion of sales in 2002, Dunkin' Donuts dominates Krispy Kreme in many categories. More specifically, the Boston-based goliath spends more money on advertising and has better name recognition, better coffee, lower-fat doughnuts, and more product offerings.[11]

However, Dunkin' Donuts' CEO Ken Kimmel has noted that, "While we are the biggest player in the doughnut business, that's not the sole focus on our business."[12] Dunkin' Donuts' product line extensions and cobranding strategies are actually being used as a model for Krispy Kreme today. And while much of the hype in the doughnut community continues to focus on Krispy Kreme, the company is well aware that Dunkin' Donuts is "thriving in their [Krispy Kreme's] backyard."[13]

Outside the Box

Einstein Brothers Bagels, a trendy bagel shop with a wide assortment of food available, is part of the much larger New World Restaurant Group and thus benefits from deep financial coffers. While the company does not sell doughnuts or offer many of the conveniences of Dunkin' Donuts or Tim Horton's, it has carved a unique niche for itself in the breakfast and lunch markets. Its food offerings are generally perceived as healthier, which has been advantageous in today's health-conscious mindset; moreover, the company has excelled with little or no advertising.[14]

Meanwhile, Starbucks is intent on developing the most recognized brand in the world, and not just in the coffee industry in which it is the dominant actor. Starbucks represents a future competitor as Krispy Kreme attempts to expand its product offering; however, Starbucks itself is characterized by a limited menu despite its wide variety of coffee flavors. With no doughnut offerings itself, it is unlikely that Starbucks will make any effort to enter Krispy Kreme's domain.[15]

HAVE YOU HEARD? YOU CAN GET THEM HOT!

Everything Communicates

The unique thing about Krispy Kreme's marketing program is that it involves virtually no advertising. "Krispy Kreme spends almost nothing on advertising. No TV commercials. No billboards. No radio ads. No print ads. They let the press give them free TV, radio, and print coverage because their store openings are so popular. Hundreds of people line up on the first day of a new store opening."[16]

On the other hand, that does not mean that Krispy Kreme is not concerned about image. "'We look at every touch point with consumers as an opportunity to brand,' says Stan Parker, Krispy Kreme's senior vice president of marketing. 'When the "Hot Doughnuts Now" neon sign is on, customers come running. You can peer through glass windows as doughnuts make their way along the conveyor belt, and the smell is irresistible. You can eat them hot. . . . That's a huge brand-building asset for us.'"[17] Moreover, Krispy Kreme utilizes a uniquely interactive employee Internet portal as a means of communicating inside out and leveraging technology to help its employees create the overall customer experience that characterizes the brand.

Segmenting Creates a Loyal Following

Krispy Kreme has generated an almost cultlike following. Many people eagerly anticipate the opening of a new store in their area, especially because the company has a policy of having only one store in an area. For example, "When it opened its first Denver location . . . doughnut fans camped out the night before, and lines extended out the door for days." The company receives nearly 5000 monthly emails from "Customers who want Krispy Kremes in their area or just want to say how much they like the doughnuts."[18] Krispy Kreme has built its insurgence around the support of this loyal customer base, which continues to be an integral part of the company's success today.

Part of the reason that Krispy Kreme's customers are described as cultlike is that the company does not seek to cater to the mass market. According to the company, "By targeting certain segments of the market, as opposed to mass targeting, Krispy Kreme is able to capitalize on those specific segments. . . . Krispy Kreme is actually in the customer satisfaction business. Krispy Kreme just happens to satisfy customers by providing a unique experience when visiting a Krispy Kreme shop, which differentiates us from the competition."[19] The company tries to focus only on its five key segments, with customers ranging from those seeking deals to those satisfying cravings, among others. This focus has helped the underdog Krispy Kreme continue its market share acquisition in the always-competitive doughnut industry.

Beyond Doughnuts

According to Krispy Kreme, "quality, service, and innovation [are the] keys to creating and maintaining a competitive advantage."[20] While the quality and service are clearly crucial to the brand loyalty that has fueled the company's success, the firm's innovative side is beginning to play an increasingly important role in revenue generation. For example, encouraged by the success of Dunkin' Donuts coffee and the continued fanatic following of Starbucks, the company launched its Krispy Kreme Signature Coffee in 2003. As one analyst put it, "They can afford to do high-end coffee now because the doughnuts are paying for the stores."[21] Other innovative programs have included pursuing partnership agreements with companies such as Wal-Mart, where Krispy Kreme has established small stores within the giant Wal-Mart superstores.

A HOT (AND COLD?) FUTURE

Many industry observers question Krispy Kreme's recent expansion
into supermarkets. According to the critics, the company's decision
is a serious threat to the Krispy Kreme brand image that has been
responsible for so much of the company's success. "By shipping their
doughnuts to a grocery store, they lose two of the most compelling factors behind the phenomenon. . . . First, the quality. . . . Second . . . [the]
Krispy Kreme experience"; as a result, Krispy Kreme may lose the
word-of-mouth promotion that is at the core of its success. Many
observers believe that "nobody [will say], 'You absolutely have to run
to the grocery store and pick up a dozen cold Krispy Kremes.'"[22] On
the other hand, Krispy Kreme's strategy has clearly been a short-term
success, with its market share of grocery store and convenience store
packaged doughnut sales increasing from 6.4 percent in 2002 to 24
percent in 2003.[23]

On the positive side, many believe that there is plenty of room
for Krispy Kreme to grow. Its more than 300 stores account for less
than 10 percent of the total number of doughnut establishments
(based on 1997 data), and its financial ratios remain strong.[24] In 2003,
the company added several new growth opportunities to its business
model, including the introduction of in-store alliances with Wal-Mart
and the acquisition of Montana Mills, which is expected to help the
company establish a network of bakery-cafe-type stores.

Notes

1. Andrew Johnson, "Overweight, Oversexed and Over Here: US Doughnuts and J-Lo Chic
   to Hit UK," Nov. 23, 2003.
2. www.krispykreme.com.
3. www.krispykreme.com.
4. Dan Ackman, "Investors Peruse Hole in Doughnut Sales," Sept. 16, 2003, Forbes.com.
5. Penelope Patsuris, "Krispy Kreme Takes a Bite Out of Britain," Nov. 14, 2002, Forbes.com.
6. Johnson, "Overweight, Oversexed and Over Here."
7. James Peters, "Sugar Rush: Krispy Kreme Rises, Challenges Segment," *Nation's
   Restaurant News,* July 9, 2001.
8. Kendra Salisbury, Western Michigan University Student Pages, "Marketing Situation
   Analysis," http://homepages.wmich.edu/~k9salisb/assign2.htm.
9. www.krispykreme.com.

10. Peters, "Sugar Rush."
11. Salisbury, "Marketing Situation Analysis."
12. Peters, "Sugar Rush."
13. Ibid.
14. Salisbury, Western Michigan University Student Pages.
15. Ibid.
16. Dan Linbach, "Has Krispy Kreme Peaked?" June 17, 2003, MarketingProfs.com, copyright 2000–2004, http://www.marketingprofs.com/3/limbach1.asp.
17. Chris Penttila, "Brand Awareness." Entrepreneurship Magazine, September 2001, http://www.entrepreneur.com/Your_Business/YB_SegArticle/0,4621,291888-1——,00.html.
18. This and the preceding quotation are from Chris Penttila, "Brand Awareness." Entrepreneurship Magazine, September 2001, http://www.entrepreneur.com/Your_Business/YB_SegArticle/0,4621,291888-1——,00.html.
19. www.krispykreme.com.
20. Krispy Kreme 2003 annual report, www.krispykreme.com.
21. Patsuris, "Krispy Kreme Takes a Bite Out of Britain."
22. Linbach, "Has Krispy Kreme Peaked?"
23. Krispy Kreme 2003 annual report, www.krispykreme.com.
24. Ackman, "Investors Peruse Hole in Doughnut Sales."

LINUX

Question: What makes Hitachi, Sony, NEC, Philips, Samsung, Sharp, Matsushita, and Toshiba, eight rivals, cooperate as they have never before? *Answer:* Linux. Linux is the open-source software that is making waves in the consumer electronics (CE) industry, waves that have even started crashing on the steps of a company its inventor watched and learned from: Microsoft. Linux's increasingly popular technology has been gaining rapid momentum as more and more companies and even state and federal governments turn to it for a lower-cost, higher-quality solution. In just a few short years, Linux has developed from an unknown operating system into a viable technological alternative in a domain that was once the sole property of Bill Gates and Microsoft.

Linux is exciting because it embodies an entire insurgent trend. Its open-source nature has created a loyal following of Linux-based designers who are using insurgent strategies to grow from underdogs to viable competitors with remarkable speed. The Linux offering is permitting a series of companies to create faster, cheaper, and, in some ways, better products for a consuming public that is looking increasingly for choice and change.

The Profile of an Insurgent:
Linux

Established:	1991
Founder:	Linus Torvalds
Availability:	Open source
Main Application:	Consumer electronics
Competing Technology:	Microsoft Windows CE
Industry Group:	CELF

Producers of Linux Software

MontaVista, Red Hat, ARM

Producers of Linux-Based Devices

IBM, Panasonic, Toshiba, Hitachi

CREATING AN OPEN-SOURCE WORLD

Finland, 1991: Linus Torvalds, a graduate student in Helsinki, develops the Linux code and makes it available through a general public license (GPL). Linux is a registered trademark, held by Torvalds, but is available to anyone or any company that wants to view its code. So, what is Linux and why is it so special?

What Is Linux?

What is interesting about Linux is that nobody really owns it, which is, of course, the whole point of an open-source program. Linux is a set of computer codes that form an operating system; it is often referred to as embedded software because it controls different devices and gadgets, but the end user does not see it at work. Linux operates under a unique system called a general public license, which, in a sense, is a legal contract permitting any company or any individual to use the registered technology and modify the codes in any way, at no charge. There is, of course, a catch: The company or developer has to make its contributions available to anyone else who wants to see them (the source code, therefore, is open). Thus, open-source technology such as Linux is designed to be continuously improved as more and more users adopt it. (Think Borg "collective" on *Star Trek: The Next Generation*.)

The primary application of Linux code has been in consumer electronics, with the current focus being on devices such as digital video discs (DVDs), video cameras, and cell phones. More specifically, Linux-based operating software is being used to drastically reduce these devices' start-up and shutdown times. And Linux-based operating software has already become common in computers and network servers.

Since Linux-based applications are not the sole property of any one company, they are in fact used by many companies. In fact, there are a plethora of intermediaries that create products using Linux code, which are then sold to end producers for use in many different high-tech gadgets. Other companies, such as the large firms mentioned earlier, will often simply incorporate Linux code into their product design for new and in-demand video cameras, faster-loading DVD players, and more versatile laptops. Linux, for its part, is also increasing in popularity in nontechnical industries, being used by companies and governments as the backbone of the general operating systems that power their networks.

The Linux Revolution

The Linux insurgence is based on several factors, most of which are related to the fact that it is an open-source product—similar, for example, to Google's search engine and Matsushita's original VHS. Individual companies are attracted to Linux because they can modify it to fit their specific needs. In fact, nearly all users find Linux attractive because it is significantly cheaper than proprietary software, such as Microsoft's. And perhaps the greatest worry for its competitors is the simple fact that Linux may be the best game in town; that is, Linux may ultimately be programmed to create faster devices, for example, than any other operating software currently in the market. As one industry insider notes: "We all love Linux. . . . There's no onerous license and no back doors or controls on how you use it. . . . This move to Linux is not just about faster boot-ups and shutdowns."[1]

A recent example of Linux's growing popularity occurred in Germany in 2003. The Munich city government chose to switch to a Linux-based operating system for all of its computers, as the system was offered at a significantly lower price than Microsoft's. Even with the personal intervention of Microsoft CEO Steve Ballmer and a drastic reduction in Microsoft's price, the Linux-based proposal from IBM-SuSE (SuSE is a German Linux distributor) won the bid (the price was about $35 million U.S. from Microsoft on its second offer compared to about $23 million U.S. from the IBM-SuSE consortium).[2] Linux is becoming increasingly popular in Asia as well; both Sun Microsystems and Alcatel have recently initiated Linux-based development programs as they expand into the region.[3]

PROPRIETARY COMPETITION

Sizing Up the Competition

What existed before Linux? In a word: Microsoft. The Redmond, Washington, Goliath—which itself invented many of this book's insurgent principles—currently offers Microsoft Windows CE, or Compact Edition. This product is a simple version of the regular Windows operating software that is today the norm on home and office computers, designed specifically for smaller devices in the consumer electronics industry. Microsoft's version, while widely acknowledged as the current market standard, is what is commonly known as proprietary software. That is, Microsoft's code is a secret, patented technology for which the company can charge a premium, with Windows CE earning nearly $40 million in revenue in 2002.

Clearly, Microsoft is studying the Linux phenomenon intensely. According to Microsoft, "The popularization of the open-source movement continues to pose a significant challenge to the company's business model. [This is] including recent efforts by proponents of the open-source model to convince governments worldwide to mandate the use of open-source software in their purchase and deployment of software products."[4] In light of the current migration toward its open-source competitor, Microsoft has made significant overtures to dissuade current clients from leaving, such as granting limited access to its secret code.[5]

So What's the Holdup?

Today, Microsoft products are stubbornly ingrained in the consumer electronics culture. While Microsoft lacks the near-monopolistic position that it created with its Windows operating system for personal and business computing in the rest of the consumer electronics industry, it maintains a very strong and important presence in that market. Moreover, since Linux is not the sole property of one owner, its support structure is not as well developed as the one available for Microsoft Windows CE.

In addition to Microsoft's strong grip on the market, several other factors have created hesitation among companies thinking about switching to Linux. Concerns have been raised about Linux's security and simplicity, the cohesiveness of the applications developed (i.e., will applications developed by one company be compatible with those developed by another), and the overall range of applications available, among other issues.[6] But as one analyst notes, "As Linux continues to prove itself in the enterprise, corporations are becoming more confident of the performance and savings that Linux offers. And with corporate support available [from companies like Dell, HP, and IBM], it provides some peace of mind."[7]

CELF-ESTEEM: RALLYING AROUND LINUX

CELF

In 2003, the eight major electronics companies listed at the beginning of this section came together to form a Linux standard-setting group to promote the continuation of Linux as an operating platform. The goal of the Consumer Electronics Linux Forum, or CELF, is to promote use of this open-source code for developing technology with greater real-time capabilities, smaller memory requirements, more effective power management, and more rapid start-up and shutdown times. More specifically, the industry organization will focus on "defining requirements for a variety of extensions in 'Linux-based CE products,' collaborating and reaching consensus with open-source projects as well as with the Linux community, thereby promoting the proliferation of CE Linux-based digital electronics in the electronics industry." IBM, for its part, has made it clear that it is strongly considering joining this industry group as well.[8] CELF is held in high esteem by many of the most successful Linux software developers, such as MontaVista Software and Red Hat.

CASE STUDIES IN LINUX

MontaVista Software

A private California-based firm, MontaVista, is making significant inroads into the consumer electronics industry. Created in 1999, it has already established a significant presence in the Linux-based embedded software industry, both in the United States and globally. MontaVista is one of the companies that turns Linux code into the software that powers the gadgets that have become commonplace in contemporary society. In early 2003, for example, the company's MontaVista Linux division introduced its Consumer Electronics Edition (CEE) 3.0 operating system, supposedly the first full-fledged Linux-based system designed specifically for consumer electronics.[9] Later in 2003, the company unveiled the latest version of its Carrier Grade Edition (CGE) 3.1, which can be used in such devices as IBM Power PCs and highly advanced telecommunications equipment.[10] MontaVista applications are sold to such firms as Alcatel and NEC, for use in their final products.[11]

Unsurprisingly, Jim Ready, MontaVista's CEO, has offered his full support for the CELF initiative: "It is wonderful that the world's leading suppliers of such devices have recognized the role of Linux in this market and are working together in the cooperative spirit epitomized by the Open Source community. Consumer electronics products have evolved into complex, multi-function, networked devices, requiring a robust and flexible operating system such as Linux."[12] The experienced CEO, who has a strong background in the embedded technology industry, feels that MontaVista and its Linux foundation are prepared to compete with the daunting competition, commenting that "Linux has emerged as a clear alternative to Microsoft."[13] The company's venture capital supporters include some of the end producers of Linux-based devices, such as IBM, Panasonic, Sony, and Toshiba (America). All eight of the founding partners of CELF license MontaVista Linux software.[14]

MontaVista: Maximizing Linux

Awards

2003:   "Best Embedded Linux Machine," LinuxUser and Developer Awards

2003:   Ranked in Top 100 Business Software companies by AlwaysOn

2002:   MontaVista Linux Professional Edition 2.1 wins "Best Embedded Tool and Development Solution for 2002" from French journal *Electronique*

2002:   *San Jose Business Journal*'s "Fastest Growing Private Companies of 2002 in Silicon Valley"

Source: Company web site.

Red Hat

This North Carolina–based company is significantly larger than MontaVista. A publicly traded company and a staunch supporter of open-source technology, Red Hat develops Linux-based operating systems that are used by firms such as Papa John's, DreamWorks, Amazon.com, Merrill Lynch, and Home Depot, in addition to working with companies such as Dell and IBM.[15]

The company feels very strongly about the detriments of proprietary technology: "In the proprietary model, development occurs within one company. Programmers write code, hide it behind binaries, charge customers to use the software—then charge them more to fix it when it breaks. No one ever has to know how bad the software really is. Bad software costs companies $78 billion per year, according to *CIO Magazine*. The problem worsens when you become tied to a company's protocols and file formats. Then you're hooked. Bruce Perens calls this the 'addiction model of software procurement.' Any model that puts customers at such a fundamental disadvantage is conceptually broken. That's why open source is inevitable."[16] At the same time, Red Hat acknowledges that at this point in the development of open-source software, the company is forced to retain a limited number of "defensive" patents on some of its applications.

Red Hat sells its operating systems on a subscription basis and also offers a host of services to its users, including consulting and support. Active in more than 60 locations worldwide and counting nearly 600 employees, Red Hat has experienced significant growth since its founding in 1993. In its 2003 fiscal year, the company had just over $90 million in revenues, up more than $11 million from 2002.[17]

Red Hat:
Leading the Linux Revolution

Awards

2002:   Red Hat CEO, Matthew Szulik, listed as "One of 20 Who Made It Possible" in *CIO Magazine*

2002:   Deloitte and Touche Technology Fast 500 (number 140)

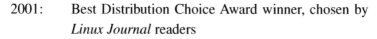

> 2001: Best Distribution Choice Award winner, chosen by *Linux Journal* readers
>
> 2001: *PC Magazine* Editor's Choice award for Best Distribution
>
> Source: Company web site.

Notes

1. "Details Emerge on Standards Group for Linux CE Products," *Warren's Consumer Electronics Daily,* July 3, 2003. Vol. 3, issue 128. New York: Warren's Communications News, Inc., 2003.
2. Michael Herman, "Battlelines Drawn," *The Christchurch Press,* July 29, 2003. Knight Ridder Tribune Business News, 2003.
3. James Niccolai, "Sun Mulls Plans to Offer Open Source App Server," *IDG News Service,* Nov. 20, 2003, http://www.arrnet.com.au/index.php?id=1324691890&fp=2&fpid= and "Alcatel Expands Broadband Strategy," China Daily, Nov. 13, 2003, http://www1.chinadaily.com.cn/en/doc/2003-11/13/content_281180.htm.
4. Herman, "Battlelines Drawn."
5. Tiffany Kary, "Update: Sony, IBM Agreement May Hurt Microsoft's Windows CE," Dow Jones News Services, July 1, 2003. Dow Jones & Company, Inc., 2003.
6. Deni Connor and Jennifer Mears, "What Users Want from Linux," Network World, Oct. 20, 2003, http://www.nwfusion.com/news/2003/1020linux.html.
7. Ibid.
8. www.celinuxforum.org/PressRelease/pr02.htm.
9. "MontaVista Software Endorses CE Linux Forum Initiative," *Business Wire,* July 2, 2003. Business Wire, 2003.
10. Company press release, Oct. 13, 2003.
11. Ibid.
12. "MontaVista Software Endorses CE Linux Forum Initiative."
13. Dean Takahashi, "Sunnyvale, Calif.-based MontaVista Software Wants Linux in Consumer Market," *San Jose Mercury News,* July 20, 2003. Knight Ridder Tribune Business News, 2003.
14. Ibid.
15. www.redhat.com.
16. Red Hat web site, www.redhat.com.
17. Red Hat 2003 annual report.

MOBILEONE SINGAPORE

MobileOne (M1) Singapore was formed in 1994 in preparation for the liberalization of Singapore's telecommunications market. With the introduction of competition in 1997, M1 experienced incredibly rapid growth, acquiring a 10 percent market share within weeks of the start of its services and quickly garnering nearly a third of the cellular subscribers within its first year of operations. Despite facing stiff competition from the incumbent operator, SingTel Mobile, the state-owned former monopolist, MobileOne was able to fill unmet demand among both residential users and business customers. The rapid and continued success of MobileOne Singapore has earned it the respect of many of its Southeast Asian competitors, through the winning of various performance and quality awards. And this regional recognition has not gone unnoticed at the international level: The British global cellular giant Vodafone recently signed a partnership agreement with M1 in its first foray into the region.

At the forefront of M1's storied, albeit short, history has been Neil Montefiore, chief executive officer and now a board member of the company (see sidebar). Credited with building the company's brand name and developing its reputation as a cellular telecom innovator, Montefiore has been a symbol of MobileOne's achievements and embodies the insurgent principles that have led the company to success—even during the telecom depression that has plagued the global market for several years.

Innovator of the Year: Neil Montefiore

Neil Montefiore, a British-educated engineer-turned-start-up-manager, has been at the heart of this insurgent company's success. With a strong background in telecommunications from his work at Cable and Wireless (a leading British telecommunications firm) and Hong Kong Telecom, Montefiore knows what it takes to achieve results in the cellular business. His strong background and widely praised managerial skills have been credited with creating an environment conducive to leading MobileOne to a rapid and triumphant entry into the Singapore mobile market. Recognized as CEO of the year by his peers in Singapore, Montefiore is characterized by his constant search for new avenues to success. When asked recently if running M1 was no longer exciting for him now that the firm had reached what many thought were unattainable heights, the chief insurgent replied, "No. The next growth engine will be visual communications. Less than one per cent of Singaporeans are using that now. It's like a startup. Nobody's done that before."*

*Angela Tan, "Eyeing the Next Big Thing," April 4, 2003, http://business-times. asia1.com.sg/story/0,4567,77421,00.html.

THE COMPETITIVE ENVIRONMENT

The World Market

The telecommunications sector, and the cellular industry in particular, was perhaps one of the largest beneficiaries of the worldwide economic expansion of the mid- and late 1990s. By the beginning of 1998, for example, there were over 200 million cellular customers worldwide—an increase of nearly 120 million subscribers in just 2 years.[1] Telecom became central to global growth. Consequently, by 2000, these companies were also at the center of a rapid economic decline, as epitomized by the WorldCom scandal.

As a result of this slower economic growth, there have been several common global trends across the maturing mobile markets of fairly developed countries. First, there is consolidation; while much of the 1990s witnessed a desire by cellular firms to tap into developing markets, the trend has since reversed, and many of the major mobile operators have begun to renew their focus on their primary markets. Second, with slower economic and related cellular growth in many of the world's congested mobile markets, operators are now forced to cut costs and look for new ways to expand. While the cost-cutting measures have many common traits, the innovation and insurgency involved in these actions are far from interesting for the most part.

More important, the constant search for new ways to generate revenue in crowded cellular markets has pushed many firms to grab hold of any new technology that was available. The most poignant example of the almost desperate quest for new revenue-producing technologies occurred at the beginning of the new millennium with the licensing of third-generation technology for exorbitant prices across Europe. Nevertheless, while some companies may have had difficulty estimating the appropriate value of new technologies, there seems to be no question that the future of the cellular market lies in data and video applications of mobile phones.

Singapore Trends

While the entry of MobileOne into the Singaporean cellular market coincided with the global telecommunications boom of the late 1990s, it also occurred just before the Asian Tigers were set back by the East Asian financial crisis of 1997–1998. Thus, while Singapore remained somewhat sheltered from the worst of the effects of the speculative financial attacks in Malaysia and Thailand, its economy was nonetheless affected by this regional destabilization. In this context, the Singaporean mobile sector rapidly became highly competitive, especially in 2000, with the introduction of a third operator, Starhub Mobile. Currently, the nearly saturated market has 3.3 million subscribers, representing a penetration level of nearly 80 percent.[2]

Today, the incumbent, SingTel Mobile, remains the largest operator, with approximately 50 percent market share.[3] M1's subscribers total nearly one-third of the market, while the new entrant, Starhub Mobile, holds the remaining share of mobile customers.[4] The regulator of the market, the Infocomm Development Authority of Singapore (IDA), has played an important role in fostering competition in the mobile sector and, according to some critics, may have played a decisive role in the speed at which M1 and Starhub Mobile achieved success.

Staking Out the Competition

MobileOne shares the Singaporean cellular sector with two other network operators. While their strategies have varied, the focus on the development of mobile technology has been a common theme for both of these MobileOne competitors. SMS (short messaging service, or text messages) and MMS (multimedia messaging service) have been crucial components of the strategies of these two companies in a common world trend and represent an important movement toward the targeting of youth. Moreover, these two messaging services are widely used by the increasingly popular prepaid market. And while SingTel Mobile has realized significant success in expanding abroad, Starhub Mobile has been trying to gather clients who have been turned off from mobile communications because of complex pricing plans and service options, as many later entrants do. Interestingly, the strategies of both SingTel Mobile and Starhub are affected by their presence in the fixed-line market. One common trend in that market has been the bundling of fixed and mobile services. Nonetheless, the two companies are formidable competition for Mobile One, and the market is often characterized by frequent pricing promotions in an effort by each company to out-price-promote, in a sense, the others.

COMPANY BACKGROUND

Starting Up: Brand Building

Montefiore led MobileOne into Singapore with the initial goal of building brand-name recognition. Having successfully achieved this goal through its "Everywhere under the Sun" campaign, M1 no longer focuses solely on brand-building directly, though it obviously takes into account the brand effect of each of its future projects. Nonetheless, "the Sun campaign was used to great effect as a vehicle to project the brand values of warmth, friendliness, reliability and creativity."[5] According to the first chairman's statement in the 2002 annual report, M1's brand image stands for "excellent customer service and support," which is its "clear competitive advantage in the Singapore mobile market."

Almost an Early Exit

Not long after MobileOne's successful entrance into Singapore's cellular market, the principal shareholders began to express concern about the future profitability of the sector and their own competence in governing a company such as M1. Thus, plans were made to sell the firm, which was then still privately owned, but the sale never occurred because of the dampened market conditions and the withdrawal of several prospective buyers. When the economy rebounded, MobileOne decided to take a new route to changing the ownership structure.

Going Public

One sure sign of MobileOne's success was its initial public offering in late 2002, which it undertook after some setbacks resulting from the previous plans to sell the firm. The IPO, however, was five times oversubscribed and was widely lauded as perhaps the year's most successful listing in Southeast Asia. In fact, it now stands as one of the largest initial public offerings in Singapore's history. And the most impressive feature of the offering, of course, was the fact that it came at a time when the economy and the stock markets were struggling in tandem, and the Singapore mobile market was reaching its saturation point. Thus, the investors clearly saw in MobileOne an ability to innovate and generate revenue that was more than impressive in what was generally viewed as a poor IPO market in 2002 (see company profile).[6]

THE LION'S SHARE OF SUCCESS

> *"To be the leader in personal communications, distinguished by innovativeness."*[7]

Striving to control the dialogue in one of the world's most competitive mobile markets, M1 has constantly changed, adapted, and offered new services to stay one step ahead of its rivals. The chairman's report notes that the firm's "focus on innovation continues to strengthen our position as the market leader in the high growth, youth and young working adult market segment." Occasionally, such innovations require working with the competition for the benefit of the industry. Innovations at MobileOne have been in the areas of technological prowess and customer satisfaction. The first 24-hour call service center for a Singapore cellular company was a product of M1's creative insurgency. Other notable firsts presented to Singapore's mobile consumers by M1 include the first GSM 900 prepaid service (1999), the first high-speed mobile data service (1999), and the first successful tests of GPRS and Wireless Access Protocol (WAP) roaming (2000), among others.[8]

The Profile of an Insurgent:
MobileOne (M1) Singapore

Facts and Figures

Formed:	1994
Operational Launch:	1997
IPO:	12/2002
Total Employees:	1453
Subscribers:	1.1 million
2002 Earnings:	$128 million
Time to Profitability:	21 months
Expected Time to Profitability:	Several years
Services offered:	GSM, GPRS, WAP, SMS, MMS, 3G (license obtained), audio and visual streaming.

The original shareholders of Mobile One—Keppel Telecoms, SPH Multimedia, and Great Eastern Telecommunications—

currently control just over 40 percent of the company, while the rest is publicly owned or held by institutional investors.

Major Awards

CEO Neil Montefiore: CEO of the year (2003); Innovator of the Year (2002)

MobileOne Singapore

1999	*Financial Times'* Global Telecoms Award for Most Effective Marketing campaign ("Everything under the Sun")
2000	Best New Operator in Asia-Pacific award by Tele.com
2001	"Everywhere under the Sun" campaign wins NY Festivals' Advertising/Marketing Effectiveness International Awards—Gold Medallion, Telecoms category

Source: MobileOne 2002 annual report and company web site. http://www.m1.com.sg/ M1/CDA/Generic_Sections/User_Guide/User_Guide_Details/1,6154,00.html?v_image =40&v_pageNumber=7.

Do the Doable

Singapore's M1 has mastered the insurgent strategy of "do the doable" by eliminating unprofitable operations. While the GSM 900-MHz system that has been in service since the company entered the market in 1997 continues to function well, M1 did not hesitate to transfer customers away from the CDMA 1900-MHz system (in operation beginning in 1998) to the GSM 1800-MHz system (in 2000) shortly after its inception. In this sense, MobileOne demonstrates an exceptional ability to use its market research and to comprehend market trends in order to shape company policy in a way that keeps up with the sector's rapid pace of technological change, but also main-

tains a streamlined product structure to maximize profitability. This insurgent tactic has helped generate much of M1's success.

"Everywhere under the Sun"

Focus on customer service has become synonymous with MobileOne in Singapore. This ability to cater to current customers' needs helps M1 hold on to its most loyal customer base.

February 2002 witnessed the introduction of a flexible service plan that was designed to keep M1's valuable youth and adult segments—for example, by empowering these customers to create personal plans centered on the use of SMS or text messages. The ability to target and maintain this soft support (soft in that these are the customers who are most targeted by M1's rivals and are most likely to switch plans given the introduction of number portability in Singapore) is crucial to M1's success.

> *"Looking ahead, the main challenge for M1 will be to sustain growth in a competitive market with high mobile penetration."*[9]
> —Neil Montefiore

How does Montefiore plan to keep M1 at its current pace? "You really have to keep services relevant to the people. Lots of things are possible now, but people won't take everything. They want things that really interest them so you have to make them relevant. That's the challenge."[10]

While other major cellular companies have begun consolidating their operations, the next big question for Montefiore and MobileOne will be whether the company will expand into new markets. While the prospect of exterior growth sounds lucrative, M1's CEO seems to be wary of the idea, warning that "companies across the world have destroyed value doing that."[11]

The final question facing M1 will be whether it can control the space on the cellular phone screen. As MobileOne adjusts to life as a public company and an established, but still insurgent, operator, it must deal with these questions while maintaining brand image and customer loyalty. The challenges ahead for this insurgent firm and its innovative leader are the challenges of an underdog company in the mobile communications field. For the foreseeable future, no company seems better positioned to dominate the competition than MobileOne Singapore does.

Notes

1. "World Cellular Growth Set to Reach 250 Million by End of This Year," *Mobile Communications*, June 11, 1998. Informa Publishing Group PLC, 1998.
2. http://home.singtel.com/investor_relations/annual_reports/default.asp#.
3. Ibid.
4. http://m1.com.sg/M1/CMA/About_Us/Corporate_Information/IR/PDF/FY2003Press Announcement.pdf.
5. Email from Chua Swee Kiat, general manager of corporate communications M1, Nov. 16, 2003.
6. Company web site, http://m1.com.sg/IR/stockinfo.jsp.
7. MobileOne annual report, 2002.
8. According to the MobileOne 2002 annual report.
9. CEO's statement, MobileOne 2002 annual report.
10. Eileen Yu, "The Top Talks," http://www.computerworld.com.sg/pcwsg.nsf/0/ 9DEDB13989 21E6AF48256B4F002AE2F3?OpenDocument.
11. Angela Tan, "Eyeing the Next Big Thing," April 4, 2003, http://business-times. asia1.com.sg/story/0,4567,77421,00.html.

NOKIA

Given Nokia's status within the world telecommunications market today, many people would not classify this mobile phone Goliath as an underdog. The Nokia story, however, is a true classic: the tale of a company that has undergone a nearly complete metamorphosis since it first began in the late nineteenth century as a wood pulp mill producing paper and power. In its relentless quest to satisfy consumer demand in a changing global marketplace, over the course of the twentieth century the company has gone from several independent companies to a multidivision international conglomerate to a focused telecommunications behemoth. Most recently, in fact, Nokia has shed many of the business lines that were formerly its primary focus. Nokia is the label on the majority of modern cellular phones as a result of the company's prudent management, resourcefulness, and constant insurgent-like focus on

consumer preferences. Moreover, it has weathered the global financial slowdown and telecommunications bust, continuing to be profitable while its competitors have faltered. This insurgent firm is one
of the most profitable and largest in Europe, despite the fact that
it is competing in a market that has existed for less than a quarter
of the company's life.

Times of Change: Nokia 1865–2003

1865:   Fredrik Idestam founds a wood pulp mill, con-
                sidered the birth of Nokia.

1898:   Finnish Rubber Works established.

1912:   Suomen Punomotehdas Oy, the first Finnish
                cable maker, founded.

1966–1967:   Merger of three Finnish conglomerates (Paper
                and Power, Rubber, and Cable) creates Nokia.

1966–1990:   Company expands globally and diversifies into a
                variety of industries, including paper, power, rub-
                ber, cable, electronics (including televisions),
                telecommunications, and information technology
                (by the late 1980s, Nokia had more than 30 dif-
                ferent business units across 10 industry sectors).

1994:   Radical consolidation of holdings. Nokia
                decides to focus only on telecommunications,
                information technology, and electronics. All
                of Nokia's founding businesses are sold or
                eliminated.

1996–1999:   Over 20,000 new employees hired, peaking in
                1999 at almost 60,000 Nokia employees (figure
                now stands at just over 51,000), more than half
                of which are not located in Finland.

2000s:	Nokia restructured into just two business groups: Telecommunications and Networks (more than three-quarters of sales are derived from telecommunication).
2002:	Top three Nokia markets are the United States, Great Britain, and China.
1996–2001:	Net sales increase from around 6.5 billion euros to just over 31 billion euros.

Source: Company web site.

FROM PAPER TO PORTABLE

A Storied History

Nokia has not always been the telecommunications leader that we know it as today. However, the firm has been characterized by an ability to adapt to changing market conditions in order to maximize profit. Listening to and identifying with consumers has allowed Nokia to construct a corporate culture that bears little resemblance to the Nokia of the past. Originally developed from a wood pulp mill and then expanding via a mid-1960s merger with cable and rubber firms, Nokia followed the late 1970s corporate trend of diversification and acquired a host of new business lines ranging from electronics to telecommunications. By the 1980s, the Finnish conglomerate had realized the growing profitability of its telecommunications line and the difficulty in managing so many different business lines. And, by the beginning of the 1990s, Nokia had narrowed its focus to telecommunications equipment supply and networks (see Nokia timeline). Today, the company is no longer involved in any of the sectors with which it made its entrance into the corporate world.

The Profile of an Insurgent:
Nokia

2002 Sales:*	30.8 billion
2002 Profit:*	3.4 billion
2003 Employees:	51,124
Stock Symbol:	NOK (U.S.)
Principal Divisions:	Telecoms and Networks

Awards and Accomplishments

2003:	Number 1 rank in Global Telecommunications Technology and European technology market in the Dow Jones Sustainability Review
2000:	World's first GPRS roaming connection, done using Nokia equipment
1998:	World's first user-changeable mobile phone faceplates
1995:	Nokia introduces world's first wireless pay phone (integrated)
1994:	First European entrant into Japanese market

*Net.
All financial data in euros.
Information above drawn heavily from Nokia 2002 annual report, www.nokia.com.

Recent Developments

By 1996, Nokia had grown to become the second-largest telecommunications equipment supplier, trailing only Motorola. That year, following a period of significant structural and strategic changes implemented by current CEO Jorma Ollila, Nokia began its ascent to the top. By 1999, the company was among Europe's largest firms and accounted for about 60 percent of the value of the Helsinki stock exchange, not to mention the fact that it had become the world's leading producer of cellular phones.[1] The firm is publicly traded on six stock exchanges around the world and has a higher market capitalization than either of its two primary rivals in the mobile phone supply business: Ericsson and Motorola.[2] With several consecutive years of multibillion-euro profits despite a sagging economy and struggling telecommunications market (and rather flat sales at Nokia itself), the company has outshined its major competitors to become a model firm.

TELECOMMUNICATIONS EQUIPMENT MARKET
Competing in a Regulated World Market

Unsurprisingly, trends and regulations at the network operator level heavily influence the telecommunications equipment industry. Despite their immense size, mobile phone providers are often at the mercy of international regulations and the demands of national operators, particularly in terms of industry standards. As a result, companies such as Nokia engage in significant and often skillful lobbying efforts at the European Union and other regulatory levels to create favorable standards that allow them a degree of certainty in their production cycles (see the discussion of Nokia's risk-taking on the GSM standard).

Industry Trends

Today, the telecommunications supply industry is affected by the global trends of increasingly mobile technology, with progressively greater importance placed on speed, data, and multimedia advancements. Moreover, the industry is affected by a tendency to be overly optimistic about the implementation of this new technology, leading many firms to create an excess supply of equipment that the market has not been quite ready to absorb. While Europe, the United States, and Japan have been the primary targets for cellular phone growth during the 1990s telecommunications boom, and even during the

2000–2001 slowdown, cellular suppliers and operators are beginning to focus on emerging markets with higher growth potential—particularly in Asia, and more specifically in China.

According to many industry observers, one of the most impressive aspects of the telecommunications expansion was the fact that it occurred, for the most part, with China remaining impenetrable to Western firms. With China's entry into the World Trade Organization (WTO), many in the industry are eagerly planning attempts to enter the world's largest single market. And the implications for telecommunications supply firms are vast. For example, in these unsaturated markets, many people will be first-time users, and the demand for equipment may lean toward simple, less expensive phones rather than the high-tech gadgets that are currently being produced for already developed sectors.[3] As a result, for these firms, the biggest industry trend will be the difficult balancing act between maintaining production for their core developed markets while tailoring product lines that are more appropriate for new opportunities in relatively immature markets.

Tough Competition

Nokia holds slightly more than one-third of the equipment supply market, sharing this market with its two primary competitors: the Swedish firm Ericsson and the American company Motorola.[4] With just over 53,000 employees and nearly 145 billion Swedish Kroner in net sales for 2002 (1 U.S. dollar = approximately 7.6 Swedish Kroner), the 127-year-old Ericsson is very similar to its Scandinavian counterpart.[5] Ericsson, however, has struggled slightly during the past several years, recognizing negative net income for both 2001 and 2002. Moreover, Ericsson maintains the same premise of focusing on customer value as Nokia, but according to some critics, it has been somewhat zealous in its recent focus on high-technology production.

Motorola Corporation, the only U.S. firm that rivals the strength of the Nordic telecommunications giants, has also faced a recent slowdown in profits and revenues. In 2002, on net sales of approximately

$26 billion this firm of almost 100,000 employees realized a net loss of just over $2 billion—its second consecutive year of negative earnings.[6] Interestingly, though, Motorola is the most diversified of the top three telecommunications equipment suppliers. And despite ailing balance sheets, both Motorola and Ericsson remain formidable competitors for Nokia.

THE KEYS TO NOKIA'S SUCCESS

The Nokia Way: "One Nokia" around the World

Nokia has made the most of Finland's advanced telecommunications market. In Finland itself, local, decentralized, and highly competitive telecommunications service companies demand continuous innovation and the highest-quality handsets from Nokia.[7] This local market, however, has become almost saturated, and, as a result, Nokia spends most of its time focusing on global operations, which cover areas from Australia to Singapore to Mexico and everywhere in between. Still, Nokia makes a continuous effort to project its stellar domestic reputation on the world scene. And with initiatives like "One Nokia" and the 1990s decision to divest all business lines except for telecommunications and networks, the company has achieved great global success. It now recognizes very little of its total revenue from its home market.

The Secret Is Youth in R&D

The Nokia research and development department has gained increasing importance from company planners in its effort to stave off the competition. It is characterized by two insurgent-like and unique elements. First, Nokia is known to have held at least one secret technology development conference, to which the company invited outside software development experts from other firms and offered them support and incentives in exchange for these firms' commitment to developing advanced Nokia technology. During this secret conference, Nokia attempted to use these outside experts to facilitate development of its Java interface technology; naturally all participants had to sign nondisclosure agreements.[8]

Second, much of the company's success has been attributed to its rather flat corporate structure, which allows even young employees to have access to senior managers. Since 1996, in large part, the firm's resurgence has been a function of an added emphasis on research and development. The combination of youth and a strong R&D focus in corporate planning has created an insurgent culture of "youthful entrepreneurship"—producing much of the rapid innovation and development that the markets have come to expect from Nokia.[9] Evidence of this continued focus on research is found in the personnel devoted to the task: While in 1996, there were only 7000 employees, that number grew to nearly 20,000 by 2003. Consistently, the company's attitude reinforces the importance of R&D for innovation: "Sustainable innovation means investing in research and development. Throughout 2001, Nokia was able to adapt quickly to a weakened market environment, sustaining good profitability and without compromising on future investments. During the year, the company increased R&D spending to EUR 3 billion (9.6% of net sales). At the end of 2001, Nokia employed 18,600 people in the area of R&D, representing 35% of Nokia's total workforce."[10]

Rapid Change

Nokia is a company that embodies change, and it bears little resemblance to the original firm of the late 1800s. In many ways, Nokia projects this image—most visibly, of course, through its product development. Thus, one of the most important benefits of the company's R&D strength has been rapid product development. In the technology business, speed is crucial, and Nokia has become remarkably adept at rapid production. For example, the company introduced 34 new products in the year 2002 alone.[11] In 1999, following Nokia's presentation of the world's first Internet-based phone using Wireless Access Protocol technology, one commentary summarized Nokia's approach: "Being the first company to introduce an Internet phone based on the Wireless Application Protocol is only Nokia's latest feat in beating the competition. Nokia also set the pace for offering sleekly styled phones, then adding functions to those appliances that were becoming fashion statements. . . . The combination of market-leading R&D and reliable production schedules is also a part of Nokia's success story. When Motorola Inc. [MOT] was late in 1997 for offering digital wireless phones in the U.S. market, Nokia filled the vacuum and hasn't allowed Motorola—or any other wireless player, big or small—to replace it."[12]

While rapid development is at the forefront of Nokia's success, it also remains one of its biggest challenges. According to the company, the recipe for continued successful innovation is a combination of "speed and flexibility in decision making, with decisions being made as close to the frontline as possible—i.e., by the most knowledgeable in any given situation."[13]

From Risk to Mix

At one time, Nokia was characterized by its ability to make profits with a minimal research and development budget. As a result, the company necessarily took some chances on its product development. And perhaps Nokia's greatest risk was its decision to focus solely on developing GSM standard phones before the protocol had acquired worldwide acceptance,[14] although it is no surprise that the company was among the many that lobbied international institutions such as the European Union to ultimately adopt the standard.

To focus on its two current objectives—telecommunications mobility and Internet Protocol advancements—Nokia devotes almost 10 percent of its revenue to R&D concentrated specifically on these two elements.[15] This current R&D focus has allowed the company to maintain an appropriate balance between high-tech development and phones that are better suited for first-time users in emerging markets. According to one analyst: "Nokia seems to have learned the product-mix lesson that Motorola and Ericsson now face. . . . If 75% of all phones are sold to first-time users, then the feature rich and Internet-access phones will be in oversupply, since most users are still learning how to use the basic features. . . . Ericsson may have gotten ahead of themselves by building these future phones when either the infrastructure isn't fully implemented, or the users aren't 'educated' in using these new features."[16]

Furthermore, part of Nokia's success has also been attributed to its early adoption of the RosettaNet supply-chain management system. RosettaNet is being adopted by many of the most important links in Nokia's supply chain, which consists of nearly 2000 companies.[17] So, recognizing that speed and scale matters, RosettaNet implementation is just another example of how the insurgent Nokia stays ahead of the competition.

CHALLENGES AHEAD

Building "a Compatible Future"

According to Nokia, "One of the greatest challenges that the wireless business will be facing in the future is that of ensuring the compatibility of different terminals, products, services and networks."[18] However, the company plans to rely on past strategies to generate future successes: rapid technology development, fueled by innovative research and development, and keen market awareness, characterized by frequent product launches and updates. In the company's own words, "The ability to continuously renew and improve our product mix while effectively managing demand/supply will be [the] key"[19] to maintaining Nokia's leader status. Only by continuously using the insurgent strategies of global brand building, effective communications, supply-chain management, and control of the telecommunications equipment dialogue through rapid product development will this underdog success be able to continue dominating the world market.

Notes

1. "Nokia's Success Story Pushing Wireless World's Envelope," *Wireless Today,* Nov. 30, 1999. Phillips Business Information, Inc., 1999.

2. "Features: Finland: Nokia's Telecommunications Laboratory," *Infotech Weekly,* Dec. 6, 1999. Independent Newspapers Ltd., 1999.
3. Bruce Gain and Darrell Dunn, "Nokia Stays Firmly on the Path while Its Competitors Stumble," *Electronic Buyers' News,* Oct. 30, 2000. CMP Media Inc., 2000.
4. www.nokia.com.
5. Ericsson 2002 annual report, www.ericsson.com.
6. Motorola 2002 annual report, www.motorola.com.
7. "Features: Finland: Nokia's Telecommunications Laboratory."
8. "Nokia's Top-Secret Developer Mission," *Wireless Week,* Feb. 4, 2002. Cahners Business Information, 2002.
9. John Blau, "Nokia Pins Its Hopes on Youthful R&D," *Research Technology Management,* September 1996. Industrial Research Institute Inc., 1996.
10. www.nokia.com.
11. Ibid.
12. "Nokia's Success Story Pushing Wireless World's Envelope."
13. www.nokia.com.
14. Blau, "Nokia Pins Its Hopes on Youthful R&D."
15. "Features: Finland: Nokia's Telecommunications Laboratory."
16. Gain and Dunn, "Nokia Stays Firmly on the Path."
17. Drew Wilson, "Nokia's RosettaNet Implementation," *Electronic Buyers' News,* Oct. 1, 2001. CMP Media Inc., 2001.
18. www.nokia.com.
19. Ibid.

PATAGONIA

In 1957, Yvon Chouinard, a consummate outdoorsman and adventurer, could not find steel pitons—safety anchors for mountaineers—that satisfied him. A self-taught blacksmith, Chouinard decided to forge new pitons himself in his backyard. He sold the extra gear he made to friends from the backseat of his parents' car, and word spread quickly that his was the world's best custom-designed climbing equipment. Chouinard's impact on the sport of climbing was enormous, allowing mountaineers to attack routes that had previously been considered inaccessible or too difficult. In 1966, Chouinard Equipment was incorporated, a company that manufactured an entire line of climbing gear, all of which carried the same branded image: "Quality You Could Bet Your Life On." And many did. By 1971, however, Chouinard realized that climbing, the sport that had inspired him all of his life, had become environmentally destructive—with pitons, his most important product, being the main source of the damage to rocks and mountains. These pitons had to be hammered aggressively into cracks and openings in cliffs and rock. So Chouinard decided to stop producing iron pitons, developing instead an aluminum chock substitute. At the same time, he became a tireless environmental advocate, changing the trajectory of his business and life forever. Chouinard's rigorous dedication to the highest quality in everything he manufactured was matched by a deep commitment, personally and professionally, to preserving the natural environment, and this ultimately defined the Patagonia brand. For example, Chouinard's promotion of the aluminum chocks in the company's 1972 catalogue included two pages detailing pitons' environmental hazards—taking control of the dialogue and having an immediate impact on the sport throughout the world. In doing this, Chouinard not only defined the Patagonia brand and the environmental future, but also inspired a new sense of responsibility in the outdoorsman community. Chouinard consistently addressed the need to "see all of our unintended consequences in everything we do," a core value that today defines him, his company, and our environmental future.

The Profile of an Insurgent:
Patagonia

Established:	1972
Founder:	Yvon Chouinard
Inspiration:	Mountaineering
	Surfing
Initial Production Facility:	Tin shack in Burbank, California
Initial Distribution:	Parents' car
Current Facility:	Ecologically designed in Ventura, California
Owners:	Yvon and Malinda Chouinard
Gross sales 2002:	$220 million

THE BIRTH OF A BRAND

The Products: Differentiation Out the Gate

In 1972, dissatisfied with the scratchy, dull, woolen clothing that was the standard for outdoor apparel, Chouinard decided to launch a clothing line that looked and felt good, but that was also functionally superior. So the Patagonia clothing line was born—named after Argentina's rugged mountains, on which he often climbed. With a fierce dedication to the quality of materials, the environmental impact of manufacturing, killer design, and functionality, the Patagonia line took the world of outdoor apparel, and urban fashion, to a whole new level. Chouinard focused on synthetic pile clothing, fleece, outdoor laminates, and light fabrics and turned them into an art form, with fleece jackets and Stand Up Shorts as his initial signature products. Once again, he innovated success, yet it was from an inner pragmatism, not a calculating business design. He actually has an unflattering image of businesspeople, men, referring to them as "greaseballs" and "dirtbags." He often says: "I'm a craftsman who just had a better idea of how to make things."

The Vision

Patagonia and the evolution it represented were based on a very clear conviction statement and mandate: "To use business to inspire and implement solutions to environmental crisis." Everyone involved in any aspect of the company, from management to employees, suppliers of source materials to subcontractors, partners to customers, all hear the same message: Patagonia not only supports environmental and social responsibility, but also literally exists because of these core values and purpose. In 1973, after Chouinard had moved his business to Ventura— to be closer to the water and one of his other passions, surfing—a local environmentalist appealed to the fledgling company for help to clean up the polluted Ventura River. The support that followed quickly became a central component of Patagonia's business; today, the company contributes 10 percent of pretax profit or 1 percent of gross sales, whichever is greater, to ecological causes worldwide. From $3 million in gross sales in 1979 to $220 million today, this "Earth tax," as Patagonia refers to it, has both made a key environmental difference and defined a powerful and differentiated brand.

The Business Model

> *"If you want to change government, change the corporations, and government will follow. If you want to change corporations, change the consumer."*

This bold statement by Chouinard, bolstered by a track record of success, performance, and quality became the foundation of a very different kind of company. Traditional wisdom might dictate that an environmental agenda is not the best path to success. But "Patagonia's environmental mission lies at the heart of the company's enduring success," writes Jim Collins, coauthor of *Built to Last: Successful Habits of Visionary Companies* (HarperCollins, 1994). Collins argues: "A company with a social agenda is more likely to succeed far into the new millennium than one that's purely revenue-driven" and "companies that consistently outperform the Dow see themselves as being much more than just about making money."

"For example," as Carol Hildebran, editor of *CIO Magazine* notes, companies like "Merck & Co. Inc. have always seen their mission as improving human health through medicine. For Patagonia, the agenda is the environment."[1]

Importantly, so as not to be hobbled by a challenging social agenda, Chouinard insists, too, on setting high financial goals and meeting projected profits. As he states: "Not to hit our profit goal is as big a problem as failing in our social mission."[2] And Patagonia's marketing, based on exciting and innovative products, drives home a sense of superior value to the customer. The company's formula: Ecological values plus unparalleled quality and style equals success.

Everything Communicates

Patagonia is constantly innovating, and it lives and breathes its success formula. It is constantly seeking ways to minimize environmental impacts and improve product quality. Soon, consumers developed a sense that there was an intangible element to the products as well— "fairy dust," as a former CMO called it. And this product meaning evolved from the company's very real commitment, throughout every phase of operations, to be different and to make a difference. For example, Patagonia recognized that "end-of-the-pipe" corporate ecology was based only on tackling problems *after* production—through cleanups, remediation, legislation, and regulation. Patagonia, by contrast, realized early on the benefits of addressing environmental impacts up front—*before* production.

To this end, Patagonia uses recycled wood and steel for its facilities, and uses nontoxic paints and natural dyes. Moreover, it produces no advertisements on billboards and uses only recycled paper for its highly regarded quarterly catalogue. Furthermore, the company developed Synchilla, a fleece fabric made of recycled soda bottles, to reduce the amount of fossil fuels used in creating commercial synthetic fleece; this alone has diverted over 150 million bottles from trash dumps over 9 years.

In 1996, Patagonia again defined the future of the garment industry when it decided to use only organic cotton for its products. This was a decision based on comprehensive research—the finding that cotton accounts for about 25 percent of the global insecticides market by value and about 10 percent of the pesticides market. In fact, the Sustainable Cotton Project (SCP) observes that 1 pound of chemical fertilizer and pesticide is required to produce the 3 pounds of cotton in a T-shirt and a pair of jeans.[3] Patagonia concluded that these chemicals have a severe impact on environmental health. And the effect of this "repurposing" has cascaded throughout the entire industry, with Nike, Levi's, and many other retailers and suppliers jumping on the bandwagon of organic cotton. Patagonia consumers, for their part, have self-identified consistently as socially responsible, active, rugged, and self-reliant. And this demographic group—part of an estimated 40-million-strong community referred to as "cultural creatives"—is a formidable, affluent, and ultimately profitable core constituency.

Notable Points of Difference

- Thirty years of an "Earth tax," 1 percent of gross sales or 10 percent of pretax profits donated to ecologically oriented nonprofits
- First designer to use fleece made out of recycled soda bottles
- One of the first U.S. corporations to offer on-site child care
- One of *Forbes's* "Best 25" Corporations in America
- An intern program that pays employees to work for an environmental group of their choice for 2 months
- Use of recycled steel and concrete and reclaimed materials for facilities
- First major apparel manufacturer to convert to organic cotton only for all product lines, 1996
- Regular supplier conferences to ensure that the entire supply chain meets environmental standards
- Q = E: Quality and environmental protection are one and the same in the company's core communications strategy for customers, employees, and designers
- First California company to commit to 100 percent wind energy use

---

Internal and External Challenges

In the 1980s, having created a unique brand of outdoor apparel and an environmental ethic, Patagonia experienced a doubling of its annual growth. It was catering not just to rock climbers and surfers, but to the full range of outdoor sports enthusiasts. Importantly, these included affluent urban dwellers with no idea of where to find the nearest mountain or surf-break. It didn't matter that they themselves did not climb high mountains or surf big waves; these consumers, soon known as "Pataguccis," were willing to pay good money for outdoor apparel.

Throughout the 1980s, Patagonia's growth came relatively easily, attributed by some to "an image and a cult of personality, which caught a big wave in the '80s, when easily smitten consumers had cash to throw at the latest trend."[4]

But during the 1990s, many cynical prognosticators became convinced that Patagonia's "tribal culture" would not survive the coming recessionary challenges. In fact, early in this decade, with a cash crunch and competitors such as Lands' End, L.L.Bean, and Eddie Bauer copying its premium products, Patagonia's growth was below expectations. For the first time, a sense of uncertainty invaded the company. And, in 1991, Chouinard faced one of his biggest career tests when he had to lay off 120 people—20 percent of the workforce, including some long-term employees. But, rather than give in to pessimism or compromise, Chouinard has vowed that his company "will increase profit, even if sales are flat, limit supply, selling to those dealers who get their preseason orders in first. Patagonia will use more local suppliers to pare costs, and it will tighten up on accounts receivable."[5]

Zen Moment

In the 1990s, Chouinard faced what he described as a "Zen moment." Given the serious business challenges, one consultant advised him, "Sell the company for a hundred million or so, retire, and if giving back is what you really yearn for, you'll have $7 to 8 million a year to give away." This was an epiphany. Chouinard and his wife realized that they had fallen into the trap of results, rather than enjoying the journey itself.

Since the beginning, the real goal for Patagonia had been the very transformation of business—to be a model of sustainable business practices and a tool for genuine social change. So, after flirtations with "professional managers" and traditional "fiscal prognosticators," the company returned to its roots, scaled back expectations, continued to innovate designs and fabrics, and soon enjoyed stable growth and profitability once again.

Interestingly, as the company rebounded, it began to believe and argue that its 40 to 50 percent annual growth rate was "excessive" and "wasteful"—that regardless of the care with which the company produced goods, it was doing damage to the environment. So, in the early 1990s, Patagonia began reemphasizing its corporate "penance"—the "Earth tax"—and expanded its efforts to mitigate any environmental damage caused by its production. This, then, was Patagonia's first order of business: scaling back growth, preventing environmental damage, and revisioning the future. Interestingly, today, consumer studies show consistently that buyers will pay a premium for products that carry a "socially responsible" label and corporate philosophy. Patagonia's ability to define the future and its own success continues.

USING CRISIS AS OPPORTUNITY

Over the last several years, with decreasing margins, aggressive competition, excessive inventory, and other industry challenges, Patagonia faced a genuine crisis of purpose and identity. Pursuing a broader market, that of general sportswear, at first struck those within the company as "selling out" and a compromise of its core purpose, "to provide technically superior products to devoted athletes and outdoor enthusiasts." But, with a deeper, broader, and more consistent market in general sportswear, profits continually increased and the company's overall health improved. Indeed, rather than a compromise on core purpose, Greenleaf Publishing concludes: "Patagonia's purpose and commitment to organic cotton has provided a rationale for making sportswear and brought about a resolution to the conflict that everyone could get behind, as all cotton used in sportswear is organic. One moral purpose has been replaced by another!"[6]

AN UNCONVENTIONAL FUTURE

Patagonia has challenged conventional wisdom and a basic tenet of business by questioning the very need to grow. Two years ago, the company's line consisted of 375 items. This year, it consists of 280 items, yet the company is doing the same volume of business. And so Patagonia's unconventional philosophy is to consume less, but consume better—for long-lasting products, durable corporate success, and long-term environmental sustainability. Patagonia, a true insurgent, continues to innovate—creating 40 to 50 new fabrics each year; seeking new ways to ensure durability, quality, and profitability; and defining a legacy with every stitch, button, and contribution to our environmental future.

Notes

1. http://www.cio.com/archive/081599_green.html.
2. Ibid.
3. *International Market News*, July 4, 2002.
4. Edward O. Welles, *Inc.* magazine, August 1992.
5. Ibid.
6. www.greenleaf-publishing.com.

RED BULL

In the early 1980s, while traveling in Asia, Austrian businessman Dietrich Mateschitz discovered a mysterious beverage, used widely by hardworking people such as rickshaw drivers in Bangkok, that provided energy and clarity of mind. Its key ingredient was the amino acid taurine, which is extracted from human and animal bile. Mateschitz tinkered with this seemingly unpalatable mix, made it into a quirky-tasting caffeinated drink, and launched Red Bull in 1987. And it has had a remarkable history, creating a mystique that feeds off a "countercultural" image—a unique marketing strategy and a rapidly growing consumer base, with sales in 2002 topping $1 billion worldwide.

The Profile of an Insurgent:
Red Bull

Established:	1987
Founder:	Dietrich Mateschitz
Product:	"Energy" beverage
First Foreign Market:	Hungary, 1992
U.S. Market Entry:	1997
Size of U.S. Market:	$350 million
Competition:	150 brands
U.S. Market Share:	65%
Global Gross Sales:	$1.2 billion

FORMULA FOR SUCCESS

The Creation of a Market

While herbal beverages and other assorted nonconventional drinks have had a relatively modest presence in the marketplace for years, Red Bull aggressively launched an entirely new category: the "functional beverage." It did this with a crafty blend of viral marketing, rebellious imagery, and sponsorship of extreme sporting events. Red Bull, in effect, was the first to market within this category, defining its own success and the new category's future. Prior to its 1997 introduction into the United States, Red Bull was already well known here through word of mouth that began in Europe. Computer programmers, technophiles, rave participants, and underground music scene players all created a "buzz" that laid the groundwork for Red Bull's North America launch. This was a deliberate tactic: creating a demand and, by design, waiting and filling it according to the company's own timetable. A Red Bull next to your keyboard, at your gig, at your club was a status symbol, and travelers to Europe were often besieged with requests from friends and associates to bring back the product. Interestingly, this approach is reminiscent of that of Coors in the 1970s, when it distributed only west of the Rocky Mountains. Colleges east of Colorado were notorious for staging "illegal beer nights," with imported bottles or cans of the "forbidden" beverage being sold for astronomical prices. In the mid-1990s, prior to its introduction into the United States, the slender, 8-ounce Red Bull can went for $5, $10, or even more to those who were lucky enough to find a can or two. A can of Red Bull currently retails for $2.

Early Adopters

Red Bull packs a powerful punch with the alleged "elixir-like" qualities of the amino acid ingredient, taurine, which some researchers contend slows the heartbeat and acts as an antioxidant to reduce free radical damage during exercise. Red Bull has a taste that approximates "liquid Sweetarts," but it acts in ways that users describe as a legal narcotic. This is not your standard thirst-quencher. And Red Bull's now well-known use as a mixer with alcohol, primarily vodka, was initially one of the first "underground" applications that swept the party world, "boosting" drinkers' moods with its volatile ingredients. Importantly, this became one of Red Bull's key "early adopter" markets, leading to its explosive growth in the United States as it flooded into the rave and club scenes. For example, the Red Bull Music Academy is a globe-trotting DJ festival in clubs in Europe, North America, and Asia—and a key part of the Red Bull "cult underground." While Red Bull claims that it does not promote its product as a mixer, it does sponsor contests and prizes for bartenders and waitresses—not to mention its "academy," which itself sponsors events in bars and clubs. A wink and a nod has become one of Red Bull's most effective marketing tools.

The "Antiproduct"

By launching the product in bars and clubs throughout Europe, Red Bull effectively seized on an antiestablishment, culturally eclectic youth market, largely defined by its stubborn avoidance of normalcy, mass media, and mainstream consumerism. Red Bull, as a pure insurgent, shunned traditional advertising—it used no billboards, print ads, or Web marketing campaigns. Instead, the company put the marketing of the product into the hands of young distributors, each armed with cases of free product, who roamed the country "turning on" their friends and throwing parties. With a logo of twin Red Bulls locking horns on a slender, chic silver can—communicating "small but effective" in a bold, "European-style" font—Red Bull transmitted a consummately hip image and now commands 65 percent of the U.S. energy drink market. Importantly, at exactly the time when dot-com corporations were lavishing and ultimately wasting hundreds of millions of dollars on television, print, and other forms of advertising, Red Bull was quietly building an empire based on the entirely different, and more cost-effective, marketing principles of the insurgent.

Brand "Elections"

As noted by Marc Gobé, author of *Emotional Branding: The New Paradigm for Connecting Brands*,[1] "Brands have to be elected to be part of the culture now." This strategy is clearly evident at Red Bull, which dispatches legions of foot soldiers in "mobile energy teams" that tote a huge can of Red Bull on the trunk—raiding college campuses, construction work sites, health clubs, and anywhere else that they can generate word-of-mouth acceptance and "votes" for their product. Recent flyers on college campuses, passed out with free cans of the beverage, state: "Red Bull stimulates brain cells and improves study." And this is how Red Bull carefully and methodically built and grew a core audience—with deliberate stealth, effective low-cost spending, and a "do the doable" grassroots marketing campaign. Not surprisingly, becoming a Red Bull brand manager is an eagerly sought after badge of honor on college campuses today.

The "X" Factor

With the banning or regulation of the product in Ireland, France, and Sweden and serious examination and discussion of it by the FDA and other regulatory agencies around the world because of perceived health threats, Red Bull has managed to cultivate an image of danger and "living on the edge." The deaths of partygoers who mixed Red Bull with alcohol, although rare and not directly attributable to Red Bull, only enhanced this image, leading youth around the world to buy even more of the product. Sponsorships of extreme, "X," sporting events—such as BMX, motocross, street luge, hang-gliding, skateboarding, wakeboarding, and bungee jumping—and quirky challenges such as kiteboard surfing contests in a "Cuba Crossing" from Key West, Florida, to Varandero, Cuba, all contribute to Red Bull's unconventional, daring brand image. Remarkably, most of these events are not at all public. In fact, they are just for the athletes: "To support a community of athletes and to bring credibility to the sports they compete in," says Emmy Cortes, director of communications for Red Bull.[2] And, in terms of attracting new customers and loyalty, "Red Bull has a more effective branding campaign than Coke or Pepsi," says Nancy F. Koehn, Harvard Business School professor and author of *Brand New: How Entrepreneurs Earned Consumers' Trust from Wedgwood to Dell* (Harvard Business School Press, 2001). Koehn continues: "Red Bull is building a beverage brand without relying on the essential equipment of a mass-marketing campaign. Perhaps the indispensable tools of marketing aren't so indispensable after all."

Controlling the Dialogue

From the very beginning, Mateschitz, who is now the richest man in Austria, developed an almost cultlike aura, refusing most interviews and controlling the dialogue, directly and indirectly. For example, Mateschitz does not attribute the creation of the beverage to any scientific analysis or expertise, preferring instead to be perceived as a beverage "shaman" of sorts, with the recipe magically springing forth from his creative mind. Red Bull shirts and logos are carefully doled out, with very few people being chosen to "wear the standard." His student "brand managers," now a virtual army, are provided with free cases of the product so that they can enthusiastically promote Red Bull to their friends, throw parties, and swap stories. Rumors of secret ingredients such "bull semen" or "bull testicles" have run rampant in this environment, while another popular "urban legend" maintained that one can of Red Bull was the equivalent of 10 cups of coffee. Moreover, the corporate web site addresses these and other safety-related issues carefully, debunking most of them: Taurine is synthetically created, not from humans or animals; the caffeine content is equivalent to that of one cup of mild coffee; Red Bull is not addictive; and it's not a doping substance. Indeed, the sheer number of disclaimers on the company's web site makes one wonder if the intent is to promote dialogue among youth, who continue to feed off of, perpetuate, and even embellish such rumors—all of which, of course, continues the Red Bull mystique and promotes sales.

THE COMPETITIVE ENVIRONMENT

Success inevitably breeds imitators. And, to date, there have been many: over 150 of them. The most notable include beverage industry incumbents: Coke immediately came out with KMX; Anheuser-Busch launched 180; Hansen's, the juice company, promotes Hansen's Red; and Pepsi introduced AMP and Adrenaline Rush, the main competitor to Red Bull, with 13 percent market share. Whoop Ass and Red Devil are among other imitators that vie for cooler space.

In addition, for years, the hip-hop world's style and trend setters for clothing and other products have gotten a buzz for entering aggressively into the energy drink business. These include Russell Simmons and his DefCon3, Ice-T's Liquid Ice, The Chronic by Dr. Dre, and Nelly's Pimp Juice, a provocative name that has resulted in boycotts and protests. ("What's next—Sambo Ham Sandwiches and Ku Klux Klan juice?" asked the Rev. Paul Scott, head of the Messianic Afrikan Nation in Durham, North Carolina.)[3]

Nelly, the highly visible rap star, is attempting to use his success in other ventures—albeit with great controversy—for crossover appeal in the energy beverage space, apparently against the advice of his own business managers, who warn that it will never work, given the size of the competition. But, with his sights on Red Bull, Nelly has persisted, even writing a hit song with the lyrics "PJ can be your sex appeal, it is your Mojo, your It factor." Additionally, Nelly is contributing a significant percentage of the profits to 4sho4kids, a foundation providing college scholarships to deserving kids—bringing a socially responsible element into the campaign as a key differentiator. And he's rolling all the dice on this one—indicative of the stakes, and potential rewards, in the space created by Red Bull.

THE FUTURE

Red Bull genuinely defined, and then seized, the market. As a result, the company continues to hold the insurgent advantage. It knows that the first mover edge is formidable, particularly when it is driven by real experiences of people identifying with tangible results from the product. Red Bull has resisted rolling out additional products in ancillary markets such as apparel and the like, choosing to remain steadfast with one product. The only exception to this is Red Bull's "sugar-free," low-carb version, a smart move in light of the Atkins craze, which shows no sign of abating.

Because DefCon3, Russell Simmons's product, is carbonated, retailers see it as a possible challenger to Red Bull—perhaps representing yet a new category: "energy soda." To date, however, it has not cut into Red Bull's dominant market share.

Ultimately, it will be interesting to see how the insurgent Red Bull manages incumbency and continues to try to rule the market it created.

Notes

1. Marc Gobé, The New Paradigm for Connecting Brands to People (New York: Allworth Press, 2001).
2. Ibid.
3. Therasa Howard, "Energy Drinks Get Their Hip-Hop On,"*USA Today*, Nov. 2, 2003.

STARBUCKS

It is difficult to imagine placing "a cup of coffee" and "revolution" in the same sentence yet, when talking about Starbucks, it can't be helped. Howard Schultz, chairman and "chief global strategist" of Starbucks, ranks among the top tier of modern-day corporate leaders who built an empire based on sweeping vision, determination, and hard work. Since buying a small, successful coffee business in Seattle in 1987, Schultz has taken the beverage world by storm, with 7000 franchises to date, a brand that some say rivals Coke, Nike, and other behemoths, and a product line that continues to grow and expand. Schultz has changed forever our everyday, benign morning sip of a "cup of Joe," transforming it into a sophisticated cultural recentering and a globally recognized experience. Orders for "lattes," "double-expressos," and "frappuchinos" are now part of the national lexicon, with a trip to Starbucks a ritual of everyday life for millions of people around the world.

The Profile of an Insurgent:
Starbucks

Founded:	1971, Seattle
Acquired by Howard Schultz:	1987
Purchase Price:	$3.8 million
2002 Revenues	$3.8 billion
Stores in Asia:	1000
Total Stores:	7427
Supports:	Fair trade coffee
	Conservation
	International literacy programs

BREWING IT UP

Humble Origins

In 1971, three academics—English teacher Jerry Baldwin, history teacher Zev Siegel, and writer Gordon Bowker—opened a cafe called Starbucks Coffee, Tea, and Spice at Pikes Place Market in Seattle, Washington. They envisioned a successful coffee business like those that had emerged in the San Francisco area, selling exotic teas and fine, dark-roasted coffees. The three believed, too, that Americans could learn to expand their horizons, to experience coffee not as a routinely undistinguished morning beverage, but rather as a freshly ground, freshly brewed, and exotic experience. The leap from store-bought canned coffee to whole-bean freshly ground coffee was a culinary paradigm shift, a "revolutionary" idea at the time. Each of the three founders invested $1350, and an additional $5000 was borrowed from a bank to open the cafe. They chose the name Starbucks in honor of Starbuck, first mate in Herman Melville's *Moby Dick*, who swilled the brew with great gusto; as reflected in the company's Mermaid logo, this name brought to mind the drama and legends of the open seas and early coffee traders.[1]

Enter the Master Marketer

Howard Schultz was vice president and general manager for Hammarplast, a Swedish manufacturer of a high-end drip coffeemaker based in New York. His sales analysis one day showed that an obscure coffee shop in Seattle was placing an enormous number of orders for that particular coffeemaker, which seemed highly unusual. Schultz decided to pay this Starbucks a visit. And from the moment he walked in the door, he was taken by the ambiance, the fresh aroma of exotic coffees, and the taste in the mug of coffee that was ground and brewed for him. A series of meetings and discussions with the three partners ensued, and Schultz was sold on their business philosophy, their dedication to customer service, and what he saw as a tremendous business opportunity selling dark-roasted, whole-bean coffee to America. So Schultz offered the three founders a well-designed plan for national expansion—and the opportunity to bring their passion, love of coffee, to a broader consumer base.

Transformation

Upon returning to New York, Schultz served Starbucks coffee to friends, who "loved the dark, rich taste."[2] He was convinced that this coffee could take the country by storm. And he began to prepare for his move to Seattle. But the call from founder Jerry Baldwin the next day stunned him: They had decided not to hire him. His ideas for expansion were viewed as too risky, too dramatic. The three original founders wanted to stay "safe" in their current trajectory. Schultz, for his part, refused to accept their decision. He passionately pleaded his case for the future of their company and for its ultimate destiny. Jerry slept on it and changed his mind and the minds of his partners, and in September 1982, Schultz took a job at Starbucks as director of retail operations. In his book, *Pour Your Heart Into It*, Schultz reflects on this moment: "In the years since then, I've often wondered, *what would have happened if I had just accepted his decision?* Most people, when turned down for a job just go away. . . . So many times I've been told it can't be done. Again and again, I've had to use every ounce of perseverance and persuasion to make things happen. . . . No great achievement happens by luck."[3] And happen it did.

Timeline

1971	• First location in Seattle's Pike Place Market
1982	• Howard Schultz joins Starbucks as director of retail operations and marketing
1987	• Schultz acquires Starbucks
	• Starbucks locations total 17

1991
- Establishes a relationship with CARE
- Becomes the first privately owned U.S. company to offer a stock option program that includes part-time employees
- Opens in Los Angeles
- Starbucks locations total 116

1990
- Completes IPO, traded on Nasdaq under symbol SBUX.
- Awarded Nordstrom account
- Starbucks locations total 165

1993
- Begins relationship with Barnes & Noble, Inc.

1995
- Awarded United Airlines account
- Begins serving Frappuccino

1996
- Opens locations in Japan, Hawaii, and Singapore
- Starbucks and Dreyer's Grand Ice Cream, Inc. introduce Starbucks Ice Cream and Starbucks Ice Cream bars

1997
- Establishes The Starbucks Foundation, for local literacy programs
- Starbucks locations total 1412

1998
- Forms Urban Coffee Opportunities, a joint venture with "Magic" Johnson's Development Corp., for underserved urban neighborhoods throughout the United States
- Signs a licensing agreement with Kraft Foods Inc. for Starbucks brand in grocery channels across the United States

1999
- Starbucks Coffee International opens locations in China, Kuwait, Korea, and Lebanon
- Forms partnership with Conservation International to promote environmentally sound methods of growing coffee

2000	•	Howard Schultz makes the transition from chairman and CEO to chairman and chief global strategist
	•	Starbucks locations total 3501
2001	•	Commits to the purchase of 1 million pounds of fair trade certified coffee
	•	The Starbucks Foundation awards more than 450 grants totaling $4.2 million to literacy, schools, and community-based organizations across North America
2002	•	The Starbucks Foundation has awarded more than 500 grants totaling $5.9 million to literacy, schools, and community-based organizations across North America since 1997
2003	•	Begins three-year $225,000 commitment to America SCORES, a national nonprofit youth development organization that uses the sport of soccer and literacy to inspire teamwork among at-risk children in urban public schools
	•	Starbucks Coffee International opens its 1000th Asia Pacific store in Beijing, China
	•	Starbucks locations total 7225

NEW VISTAS

GQ *Meets Grunge*

The culture shock of a New York, Armani-clad executive in the laid-back, casual Northwest was significant, but not insurmountable. Schultz's pleasing manner, professionalism, and savvy marketing skills were obvious. Yet, he needed a break, which came one day when he literally leapt over the counter and chased a thief who had walked out with two expensive coffeemakers, screaming, "Drop that stuff!" The thief complied. And Schultz retrieved the merchandise, to onlookers' great applause. Later that day, the staff erected a banner reading: "Make My Day!" And so Schultz's policing skills soon began to feed into his real abilities: insurgent marketing and promotion. For example, Schultz noticed that many customers were either unfamiliar or uncomfortable with the new coffee experience, and at times were treated with an aloof attitude by more knowledgeable patrons and servers. Schultz's response was to develop a customer relations protocol and educational brochures to eliminate this barrier to progress. He created an attitude of inclusivity and made it a core value of the company.[4]

Bella Italia

In 1983, on a housewares show trip to Milan, Schultz was overcome by the richness, pleasure, and cultural vibrancy of espresso bars in Italy. Here was a "third home" where people met, relaxed, interacted, and enjoyed the theatrical preparation of espresso and "caffe latte." This was unknown in America. Schultz decided to bring all this back with him—and to make Starbucks a genuinely differentiated experience, far more than just brew and beans and the selling of coffeemakers. Once again, Schultz genuinely wanted to share the experience his customers were missing in America.[5]

New Incumbent Resistance

Despite the overwhelming success of a Starbucks espresso bar trial, the three original founders, comfortable with their current success, balked at "compromising" their core business of selling coffee. The three founders were concerned that this might get them into the "restaurant business." And in late 1985, Schultz, remaining on good terms with the founders, left Starbucks.

IL GIORNALE

Schultz launched Il Giornale, a coffee-bar venture—ironically, Starbucks, which put in $150,000, was the first investor! Jerry

Baldwin also agreed to be on the board of directors of the new company, and Gordon Bowker was hired as a consultant. Raising the $1.6 million in capital was very difficult, with most investors citing declining coffee consumption and questioning if people would pay $1.50 for a cup of Joe. Nevertheless, in April 1986, the money was raised and the first Il Giornale opened, with Italian opera music, European décor, and espresso makers in white shirts and bow ties. It was an immediate hit, with three stores grossing $1.5 million within 1 year. In August 1987, Schultz, at age 34, bought Starbucks from the partners, all of whom wanted out for various reasons, for $3.8 million. He was now president and CEO of Starbucks Corporation.

BRAND BUILDING

Schultz's vision was for Starbucks to become a national company with a corporate culture that everyone could be proud of. Sharing success, embracing corporate social responsibility, and promoting the best products possible all led the company to long-term value and victory. The Il Giornale and Starbucks logos were blended, as were the styles of the two chains, producing a new hybrid establishment that was part coffee shop, part espresso bar.

Today, of course, Starbucks' entire ambiance has succeeded brilliantly—the open spaces, attractive packaging, congenial staff, curved bars, and friendly lighting. Early on, Schultz realized that it's more than just the coffee. Indeed, this was the essential lesson that he learned in Italy and re-created in classic American style; some people today even describe Starbucks stores as an "urban oasis." Everything from napkins to floor tiles to products to aromas communicates in the *same* direction and defines the brand and the company. Schultz, for example, is fond of saying "retail is detail." And store design teams actually number over 100 people who constantly seek new ways to respond to customer attitudes and feedback—and to improve Starbucks' image, responsiveness, and resilience.

THE FUTURE

A Restless Incumbent

With constant additions to its product lines—including mail order prod-ucts, vendor contracts with *Fortune* 100 companies, supermarket sales, CDs, ice cream, and packaged frappuchinos—Starbucks is constantly on the move. It has a genuine commitment to a wide range of socially responsible programs, and annual revisiting of values and principles and attention to the bottom line has become the company's norm.

In late November 2003, Starbucks stock traded at an all-time high of $33.00 per share. Currently, Starbucks has 2600 stores equipped with wireless Web access, a move the company made in spite of analysts' predictions of a severe drop in revenue per customer at public access points. Schultz, in fact, notes that the company's $410 million in revenues in June 2003 is a 27 percent increase from last year—a spike that he attributes to wireless technology.[6] Schultz, always plugged in, remains a restless incumbent who leads his com-pany like a classic insurgent.

Notes

1. http://www.mhhe.com/business/management/thompson/11e/case/starbucks.html
2. Howard Schultz, *Pour Your Heart into It*. New York: Hyperion Press, 1997.
3. Ibid, p. 44.
4. Op Cit http://www.mhhe.com/business/management/thompson/11e/case/starbucks.html.
5. Ibid.
6. http://www.time.com/time/2003/wireless/article/starbucks_unwired_the_c01_print.htmlu.

Index

About the Authors

David Morey is founder, president, and CEO of DMG, a leading strategic communications consultancy. He is an adjunct professor of international affairs at Columbia University and served recently as a chairman of the Council on Foreign Relations' Task Force on Public Diplomacy. His political clients include Corazon Aquino, Kim Dae Jung, Chen Shui-bian, Virgilio Barco, Boris Yeltsin, and Vincente Fox. His Fortune 500 clients include Verizon, The Coca-Cola Company, Microsoft, Nike, KPMG, McDonald's, Visa, Procter & Gamble, Texas Pacific Group, Reebok, J. E. Seagram, Hughes, News Corp., Allied Domecq, Bancomer, and many others.

Scott Miller is the president and founder of Core Strategy Group in Atlanta, Georgia. He was founder of the pioneering political consulting firm Sawyer/Miller Group in New York. Among Sawyer/Miller Group's clients were Corazon Aquino, Vaclav Havel, Boris Yeltsin, Kim Dae Jung, Virgilio Barco, USA for Africa/Hands Across America, Lech Walesa, The Better World Foundation, over 40 U.S. candidates for governor or senator, and every Democratic presidential candidate from 1976 through 1988.

Core Strategy Group's corporate clients have included McDonald's, Verizon, CitiGroup, Microsoft, The Coca-Cola Company, News Corp., The Tribune Company, Highfields Capital, Cox Enterprises, Women & Co., Knight-Ridder, The Southern Company, Janus Capital Group, The Home Depot, The Boston Beer Company, and Disney.

Please visit our web site, www.UnderdogAdvantage.com, and feel free to e-mail any questions or comments.